A Most Unlikely God

A Most Unlikely God

*A Philosophical Enquiry
into the Nature of God*

BARRY MILLER

University of Notre Dame Press
Notre Dame and London

BT
102
.M553
1996

Manufactured in the United States of America

Library of Congress Cataloging-in-Publication Data

Miller, Barry, 1923–
    A most unlikely God : a philosophical enquiry / Barry Miller.
      p. cm.
    Includes bibliographical references and index.
    ISBN 0-268-01422-1 (alk. paper)
    1. God.   I. Title.
  BT102.M553 1996
  211 — dc20   95-50518
                                        CIP

∞ The paper used in this publication meets the minimum requirements
of the American National Standard for Information Sciences — Permanence
of Paper for Printed Library Materials, ANSI Z39.48–1984.

Book design by Will H. Powers
Typesetting by Stanton Publication Services, Inc., St. Paul

Contents

Preface

In *From Existence to God* I argued in some detail for the existence of a creator of the Universe, leading one reviewer to concede that the cosmological argument may well have been shown to be free of 'what looked like some serious obstacles.'[1] He was quick to add, however, that there still remained a very substantial journey 'from uncaused cause to the worship-worthy God of Christian religion,' a journey which he himself regarded as problematic. The present work is an attempt to traverse a large part of that journey by drawing out some of the radical implications that the conclusion of the earlier work has for a philosophical understanding of the divine nature.

One of the main obstacles to such an understanding is the unfortunate influence of what has become known as 'perfect-being' theology, a philosophical theology which starts from the notion of God as the absolutely perfect being, and proceeds to infer that such a being has all the properties that it is better to have than not to have. Moreover, he has them all to the maximum degree possible. On this view, God is like some of his creatures in being powerful, knowing, good, and so on. He is unlike them, however, in having each of these properties to the maximum degree, and thus is said to be all-powerful (omnipotent), all-knowing (omniscient), all-good (omnibenevolent), and so on. It is indeed easy to see why many might regard such a view as hard to fault, and all the more so when it is formulated at this level of generality.

I do fault it, however, not because it attributes too much to God, but because it attributes far too little. For the creator of the Universe, even the maximum degree of all the great-making properties is not enough. For him, even the maximum degree of all the great-making abilities and capacities is also not enough. All these might well be more than enough for a perfect human being, and they might even be exactly right for any creature that was a perfect

1. R.W. Hepburn in *Mind* 102 (1993): 674–76.

pure spirit. They are far from right, however, for the perfect being who created the Universe. He is simply not like that at all; and perfect-being theology
does him a great disservice in suggesting that he is. Just what he really is like,
and how radically he differs from even the most exalted of his creatures is the
subject of this book.

In writing the book I am much indebted to comments from David Burrell,
Fred Crosson, Peter Forrest, Fred Freddoso, Bruce Langtry, Brian Leftow,
Michael Loux, Phillip Quinn, and Stephen Voss.

Easter Day, 1995

A Most Unlikely God

1

Discordant Views of God's Nature

A time-honoured procedure for discussing God's nature[1]—what he is like, how he differs from creatures—has been to settle upon some controlling notion to use as the yardstick against which to judge what can or cannot be said of God. For contemporary perfect-being theologians, or Anselmians, that notion has been of God as the perfect being, for Moses Maimonides the notion of God as One, for Aquinas the notion of God as Subsistent Existence, and for Leibniz it seems to have been a matter of indifference as to whether he used the notion of a perfect being (as he did in connection with his ontological argument) or of a First Cause (as he did in connection with his cosmological argument). With this general procedure I have no quarrel, and shall in fact be using it myself. There are, however, two obvious ways in which it can go wrong. One is in the choice of the controlling notion, and the other is in the application of that notion to specify the divine attributes. Since perfect-being theologians, or Anselmians, provide an example of the first mistake, and negative theologians of the second, it will be instructive to examine each of them before attempting to tread once more the path along which even some eminent thinkers have often stumbled.

Perfect-Being Theology

In challenging the controlling notion of God employed by perfect-being theologians, I have no wish to deny that he is indeed the absolutely perfect being. What I shall be denying, however, is their particular understanding of that notion. Aquinas, for example, understands a perfect being as Actus Purus, a being devoid of all potentiality; Maimonides conceives of it as One, a being

---

1. True, Alvin Plantinga has concluded that God has no nature. Cf. his *Does God have a Nature?* (Milwaukee: Marquette University Press, 1980). Later, however, I shall be arguing that his case is vitiated by a serious misunderstanding of the divine simplicity.

'without any composition or plurality of elements'; but Anselmians understand it as a being having the maximally consistent set of great-making properties or perfections. Whether the Anselmians' view is acceptable, however, depends on what they mean by a perfection. As explained by Morris, it is a property that fulfils the following conditions:

1.01.   It is better to have than not to have.
1.02.   It may vary in degree.
1.03.   It is 'constituted by the logical maximum of an upwardly bounded, degreed great-making property.'[2] Omnipotence and omniscience are offered as examples.

The procedure for determining which great-making properties belong to God could hardly be simpler, namely, if having property P 'contributes to the excellence of a thing that does have P, then an absolutely perfect being has P, otherwise the being does not have P.'[3] Among those that pass the test are omnipotence, omnibenevolence, omniscience, and indeed all the perfections.

The Anselmians' notion of a perfection has immediate implications for their understanding of God's transcendence over his creatures. They succeed in setting him well apart from his creatures, many of which may perhaps have great-making properties but no one of which would have even one of them to the maximum degree possible. On this view, the gulf between God and creatures would therefore be wide, and perhaps unimaginably so, though it would not constitute an absolute divide. It is difficult to see how it could be more than a difference of degree, since the terms indicating his properties — 'powerful,' 'knowing,' 'loving,' 'merciful,' 'generous' and so on — seem to be used univocally of God and creatures. True, when applied to God, those terms are often qualified as '*maximally* powerful,' '*all* knowing,' '*infinitely* merciful,' '*unsurpassably* generous,' but the qualifiers do nothing to change the sense of the terms they qualify. Hence, the role of 'maximally,' 'all,' 'infinitely,' and 'unsurpassably' cannot be that of *alienans* adjectives[4] like 'decoy' in 'decoy duck,' or

2. T. Morris, *Anselmian Explorations* (Notre Dame: University of Notre Dame Press, 1987), 21.

3. G. Schlesinger, *New Perspectives on Old-Time Religion* (Oxford: Oxford University Press, 1988), 16.

4. An *alienans* adjective is an adjective which changes (i.e. alienates) the sense of the nouns it qualifies, as is evident from the examples in the text. From the fact that an object is a decoy duck, one cannot infer that it is a duck, though that is just what one could infer from the fact that an object is a brown duck. Again, one cannot infer that the phenomenon of negative growth is growth, though one can indeed infer that fast (or slow, or erratic) growth is growth. On a number of occasions throughout the book I shall have occasion to draw attention to the importance of recognizing some adjectives as alienans ones.

'negative' in 'negative growth,' each of which does serve to change the sense of the term it qualifies. Rather, they are merely superlatives, which of course leave quite intact the sense of the terms they qualify. Thus understood, God's properties are merely human ones, albeit extended to the maximum degree possible.[5]

As conceived of by perfect-being theologians, therefore, God turns out to be simply the greatest thing around, some kind of super-being that would be quite capable of evoking admiration and wonder, but who could scarcely be described as being absolutely transcendent, or as being worthy of worship. The point is that the terms that perfect-being theology predicates of God are being used in precisely the sense that ipso facto precludes their being predicated of a God who is *absolutely* transcendent, since it is a sense in which they could equally be predicated of creatures. The difference between creatures and any God of whom they really could be predicated would therefore be simply one of degree. Although this may seem to be a hard saying, it follows straightforwardly from the fact that absolute transcendence cannot be attained merely by extending human attributes to whatever degree is deemed to be 'maximal.' The Anselmians' God is therefore anything but ineffable, for not only can we talk about him, we can do so in precisely the same terms as those we use in talking about humans. Such a view succeeds in presenting God in terms that are comfortingly familiar, but only at the price of being discomfitingly anthropomorphic.[6]

The Anselmians' notion of a perfect being has been presented as reflecting Anselm's own notion of God as 'that than which nothing greater can be conceived.' Underlying that suggestion, however, is the assumption that greatness

---

5. Although differing on many issues, process theologians and perfect-being theologians seem to be in broad agreement on at least two points, namely, the procedure for determining the (material) attributes, and the fact that such attributes are maxima. Thus, on the first point D. Pailin writes: 'The guiding criterion [for determining which material qualities are to be attributed to the divine] is that suggested by Anselm's perception that, as "the supreme Good through which every good is", God must have every good and so be "whatever it is better to be than not to be"'(p. 75). On the second point, he notes that 'although . . . it may not be possible to comprehend what it is to be "perfectly" loving, such a description suggests that in this respect God is to be considered as the ideal terminus of the range from hating to loving and from the less to the more loving' (p. 27). D. Pailin, *God and the Processes of Reality* (London: Routledge, 1989).

6. A view of God that differs to some extent from that of perfect-being theology is one that depicts at least some of God's properties as differing from human ones not merely in degree, but by way of specific difference. This view, however, is far from avoiding anthropomorphism altogether, since at least some divine and human properties would still be generically the same. William Alston is an advocate of this view in his "Divine and Human Action" in T. Morris, ed., *Divine and Human Action* (Ithaca: Cornell University Press, 1988), 259–80.

in any respect is to be understood in terms of a scale of more and less, with the greatest being at the maximum on that scale. Although the unfortunate consequences of the assumption are now apparent, it might well be asked whether it was unavoidable. Was there really any alternative? In fact, the alternative was to consider the possibility of the greatest being as not restricted to lying *on* any scale whatever — not even at the summit — but as that to which the items on the scale merely *point* or that towards which they merely tend to converge without ever actually doing so. In other words, what should at least have been considered was the possibility of the greatest *F* not being the final member in a series of members that were *F* to an increasing degree, not belonging to the series at all, but lying completely *outside* it. In that case, the greatest *F* would not be a maximum or limit *simpliciter* in an ordered series of *F*s, as Anselmians understand it to be. Rather, it would be the limit *case* of such a series. This is a distinction which I shall explain shortly, but only after indicating why perfect-being theologians are not the only ones to ignore it: negative theologians are no less at fault.

Negative Theology

At the opposite pole from perfect-being theology is the negative theology exemplified by Moses Maimonides, some of whose remarks make perfectly clear how he would respond to the claims of perfect-being theology:

[It should be said] that those who believe in the presence of essential attributes in God, viz., Existence, Life, Power, Wisdom, and Will, should know that these attributes, when applied to God, have not the same meaning as when applied to us, and that the difference does not only consist in magnitude, or in the degree of perfection, stability, and durability. It cannot be said . . . that His existence is only more stable, His life more permanent, His power greater, His wisdom more perfect, and His will more general than ours, and that the same definition applies to both. This is in no way admissible, for the expression "more than" is used in comparing two things as regards a certain attribute predicated of both of them in exactly the same sense, and consequently implies similarity [between God and His creatures]. When they ascribe to God essential attributes, these so-called essential attributes should not have any similarity to the attributes of other things, and should according to their own opinion not be included in one of the same definition, just as there is no similarity between the essence of God and that of other things. . . . the terms Wisdom, Power, Will, and Life are applied to God and to other beings by way of perfect homonymity, admitting of no comparison whatever.[7]

7. *The Guide for the Perplexed*, trans. M. Friedlander (New York: Dover Publications, 1956), 79–80.

The striking contrast between Anselmians and Maimonides in their under-standing of the divine attributes reflects the chasm between their controlling notions of God, the former insisting on their idiosyncratic notion of what a perfect being should be, and the latter conceiving of a perfect being as 'one in every respect, containing no plurality or any element superadded to His essence.'[8] In saying that God is one, however, Maimonides is not attributing anything real and positive to him, for 'God's unity is not an element super-added, but He is One without possessing the *attribute* of unity.'[9] Rather, he is saying merely that 'there cannot be any belief in the unity of God except by admitting that He is one simple substance, without any composition or plu-rality of elements; one from whatever side you view it, and by whatever test you examine it; not divisible into two parts in any way and by any cause, nor capable of any form of plurality either objectively or subjectively.'[10] From this, Maimonides concludes that in God there can be no positive attributes at all: 'God's existence is absolute. . . . Consequently, it is a false assumption to hold that he has any positive attribute.'[11]

What, then, is to be made of the variety of attributes that we do in fact as-cribe to the God who is One? How do they square with the 'lack of plurality' upon which Maimonides insists? In his view, the multiplicity of ascriptions reflects no plurality in God himself but only in his *effects*. For example, be-cause wisdom and power in creatures are distinct divine effects, we may say that God himself is wise and powerful, though not meaning that he is in any way similar to those disparate effects, merely that he is *not* unwise and *not* powerless. That the divine wisdom in itself and the divine power in itself are not distinct from the divine essence is something that must be affirmed, even though this lack of distinction utterly transcends all human understanding.

All this having been said, it has nevertheless to be recognized that a nega-tive theologian could quite consistently make such affirmations as 'God is powerful and knowing and willing,' provided that it were interpreted not as a triple affirmation of what God is but merely as the triple *denial*, 'He is neither powerless, not inattentive, nor negligent.' Similarly, to say that God is wise or merciful or intelligent would be to say that neither human wisdom, nor human mercy, nor human intelligence bears any resemblance to anything to be found in God. Indeed, no real property could legitimately be attributed to God except it be understood in these purely negative terms:

8. Ibid., 72.
9. Ibid., 80. My emphasis.
10. Ibid., 69.
11. Ibid., 82.

Since it is a well-known fact that even that knowledge of God which is accessible to man cannot be attained except by negations, and that negations do not convey a true idea of the being to which they refer, all people, both of past and present generations, declared that God cannot be the object of human comprehension, that none but Himself comprehends what He is, and that our knowledge consists in knowing that we are unable truly to comprehend Him.[12]

In regard to what God is, therefore, Maimonides holds that we are irredeemably ignorant. This view is not restricted to some mediaevals but has much in common with the contemporary Keith Ward's 'fairly radical agnosticism about the being of God,' and his claim that 'one characterizes God in the way which evokes an appropriate attitude in man, not in the way which describes his inner being most correctly.'[13]

Finally, lest negative theology be misunderstood as denying *all* positive properties to God, we should be clear that it denies only those that are real rather than Cambridge.[14] Thus, such positive attributions as 'God was worshipped by the Israelites' or 'God is praised by some people, but derided by others' are quite acceptable to negative theologians; for being worshipped, praised, or derided are properties that need make no difference whatever to their objects. Nor, in the opinion of many mediaeval philosophers, are God's creating, sustaining, or intervening in the Universe any more than merely Cambridge properties: they are said to make no more difference to him than his being worshipped or praised. Since Maimonides himself was of that view, he would have no objection to such positive attributions as 'God is the creator of the Universe' or 'God is the sustainer of the Universe' or 'God brings about such-and-such in the Universe.'

Negative theologians and Anselmians have now presented us with two radically opposed notions of God and his attributes. On the one hand, there is a God so lacking in plurality as to be marked by no internal distinctions whatever; on the other hand, a God so riven with distinctions, so character-

---

12. Ibid., 84–85.

13. K. Ward, *The Concept of God* (Oxford: Blackwell, 1974), 156–57.

14. This point is overlooked by Morris (*The Concept of God* [Oxford: Oxford University Press, 1987], 11) in his attempt to show that negative theology is 'self-defeating', on the grounds that at least one property is shared by God and humans, namely, 'the property of having properties not shared by some being with a different ontological status.' Since this property is merely a Cambridge one, negative theologians can acknowledge it without any inconsistency.

ized by plurality, as not to be identical with all his attributes, nor they with each other.[15] On the one hand, a God so far from being anthropomorphic as to be shrouded in the negations of human properties; on the other hand, a God so anthropomorphic as to be describable by predicates which remain basically human ones, even when qualified by the likes of 'maximally' as in 'maximally wise' or 'omni' as in 'omniscient' or 'unsurpassably' as in 'unsurpassably generous.'

I remarked earlier that perfect-being theology is an example of what happens when one's thinking about God is controlled by a notion of him that is defective. In Maimonides' basic notion I find no defect, and shall in fact be defending it against those who regard it as thoroughly objectionable. The defect I do find in him is merely with the use he makes of that notion, not with the notion itself. In assuming that God's absolute transcendence precludes our ascribing any real properties to him, Maimonides ignores the fact that there is at least some similarity between a limit case and its corresponding limit simpliciter or maximum, notwithstanding the absolute difference between them. Despite the radical opposition between Maimonides and the Anselmians, therefore, the flaws in their positions have at least one common root, namely, their neglect of the distinction between limit simpliciter and limit case, a distinction that hitherto I have merely mentioned but shall now explain.

Notions of Limit Simpliciter and Limit Case

A basic difference between a limit simpliciter and a limit case is that the former differs merely in degree from that of which it is a limit simpliciter, whereas the latter differs absolutely from that of which it is a limit case: the limit *simpliciter* of an *F* is an *F*, whereas the limit *case* of an *F* is decidedly not an *F*. Consider, for example, the speed of moving bodies. As we are told, the upper limit on their speed is the speed of light. This is a limit simpliciter. Although we might be inclined to think that their speed has also a lower limit simpliciter (0 km/s), we should be wrong, for it is merely a limit case. Indeed, there is no lower limit simpliciter, since there is no speed below which there could not be a still lower speed. An obvious difference between the lower limit case and the upper limit simpliciter of the speed of moving bodies,

---

15. Only a few perfect-being theologians would deny these distinctions, though, in my view, such denial is not consistent with perfect-being theology.

therefore, is that the upper limit simpliciter is indeed a speed (300,000 kms per second) whereas the lower limit case is not a speed at all.

First-level predicables provide a further example of this difference. It may be theoretically possible, even if practically useless, for them to have any number of gaps. Purely for purposes of illustration, however, we might restrict the gaps to four. In that case we could have the following series:

4-place predicable, 3-place predicable, 2-place predicable, 1-place predicable

A 1-place predicable is a limit not because its gap is ineliminable, but because any expression formed by eliminating the gap would not be a predicable in any univocal sense of that term. A 1-place predicable is that member of a series of predicables beyond which no expression could be a predicable: it is a limit simpliciter. Nevertheless, we can see perfectly well what would happen if that last gap were in fact to be eliminated. The resulting expression has sometimes been called a 'zero-place *predicable*' even though it is no more a predicable than negative growth is growth.[16] It is in fact a proposition, albeit one that is logically simple in the sense of having no *sub*-propositional parts whatever.[17] By eliminating the last trace of what makes a predicable a predicable, we get an expression that is not a predicable but an expression with a truth-value, namely, a proposition. This is a *limit case* predicable: unlike the limit simpliciter, it is not a member of the series of which it is the limit case. However, although not belonging to the series, it is not totally unrelated to the members, since it is they and the way in which they are ordered that point to this limit case: although different in kind from the series' members, it is that towards which those members do point.

Similarly in regard to a point: although differing in kind from the ordered members of a series of ever shorter lines, it is that towards which the series points. Similarly, too, in regard to a line, since it differs in kind from the ordered members of a series of ever narrower surfaces, but is that towards which the series points. Similarly again in regard to a circle, since it differs in kind from the ordered members of a series of regular polygons[18] with ever

16. As used in 'zero-place predicable' and in 'negative growth', the terms 'zero-place' and 'negative' are functioning as *alienans* adjectives.

17. Cf. my "Logically Simple Propositions," *Analysis* 34 (1974): 123–28, where I argue that it is not contrary to the nature of propositions that some should have no sub-propositional logical parts (neither subject nor predicate, first-level predicable nor second-level predicate), and where I offer some everyday examples of such propositions. For a briefer account, see the Appendix to chapter 8.

18. A polygon is regular if all its sides are equal. Otherwise, it is irregular.

more sides, but is that towards which the series clearly points. Thus, the limit case of a line is not a line but a point, the limit case of a surface is not a surface but a line, the limit case of a regular polygon is not a polygon but a circle, and the limit case of a series of first-level predicables is not a predicable but a proposition.

It may now be intuitively, even if obscurely, evident what would count as a limit case and what would not. In an attempt to dispel something of the obscurity, let me list the various series for closer examination:

1.04.   . . . 4-place predicable, 3-place predicable, 2-place predicable, 1-place predicable. The limit case is a zero-place predicable (a proposition).

1.05.   regular polygon with sides turning by 360/3 degrees at its vertices, one with sides turning by 360/4 degrees, one with sides turning by 360/5 degrees, . . . one with sides turning by 360/n degrees. . . . The limit case towards which these polygons converge is one in which there are *no* angles (a circle).

1.06.   1 metre line, .5m line, .25m line, .125m line. . . . The limit case is a 0m line (a point).

1.07.   1m-wide surface, .5m-wide surface, .125m-wide surface. . . . The limit case is a 0m-wide surface (a line).

About the first series it is clear that no member is either more or less a predicable than any other member, nor is any member of the second series either more or less a regular polygon that any other, and similarly for the other series. In general, a series of *F*s is ordered according to the *degrees* of *F*-ness had by its members, which are all equally *F*. In no case, however, can the limit case be a member of that series, for it is not an *F* at all.

What, then, is the basis on which the members are ordered? They are ordered according to variations in a defining characteristic. A defining characteristic of a first-level predicable is that it be attachable to one or more proper names to form a proposition. A defining characteristic of a regular polygon is that it be equal-sided or equiangular, of a line that it have length, of a surface that it have breadth. Note, therefore, that the first series is ordered according to variations in the number of proper names required to form a proposition with the predicable, the second according to variations in the number of sides or in the sizes of its angles, the third according to variations in length, the fourth according to variations in breadth.

And what is the limit case in such series? In each one of them it is that in which a defining characteristic of the members has been varied to the point of extinction; and an *F* from which a *defining* characteristic is absent is obviously not an *F* at all. In general, if there is a limit case to an ordered series of instances of *F*, the limit case itself will not belong to the series, for there will be an absolute difference between it and the members of that series. It will no more be an instance of *F* than a rocking horse is a horse, or negative growth is growth, or a decoy duck is a duck. Consequently, the term 'limit case' in 'limit case instance of *F*' functions as an *alienans* adjective like 'rocking' in 'rocking horse'. 'Limit simpliciter,' on the contrary, is *not* an alienans adjective in 'limit simpliciter instance of *F*.' Likewise, the term '1-place' in '1-place predicable' is not an alienans adjective, although the term 'zero-place' is.

To have understood the discussion of limit cases is to have understood that the absolute difference between the members of a series of *F*s and their limit case does *not* entail that the relationship between them is merely a matter of convention. Clearly it is not; otherwise, there could be no objection to allowing the limit case of a series of *F*s to be interchangeable with the limit case of a series of *G*s, e.g. that the limit case of a series of predicables be interchangeable with the limit case of a series of polygons. Precisely this non-interchangeability makes it clear that there is at least some similarity between a limit case of a series and the members of that series.

In failing to understand that there is some kind of similarity between members of a series and their limit case, perfect-being theologians and negative theologians alike have ensured the falsity of their claims about the nature of God. Perfect-being theologians did so by ignoring the possibility of there being anything similar to, but *beyond*, the maximum of a series of *F*s. Maimonides did so by not recognizing the possibility of some *likeness* between that entity and the members of the series beyond which it lay.

An obvious lesson to be learned from the errors of perfect-being theology and negative theology is that no enquiry into the divine nature can afford to repeat their sins of omission. On the contrary, any notion that is assigned the controlling role in our understanding of God will have to be one that does justice to the distinction between limit cases and limits simpliciter. Is there such a notion? I shall be arguing that there is, and that it is in fact the notion of a God whose role as creator of the Universe requires that he be identical with his existence. This is the classical notion of God as *ipsum esse subsistens* or Subsistent Existence, for whose existence I argued in *From Existence to God*. It is also, by implication, the notion of a God who is simple. And, as I shall be arguing in the present work, although the notion of a simple God admittedly makes no sense whatever in terms of limits simpliciter, it makes perfectly good sense in terms of limit cases.

Divine Simplicity

What, then, is the doctrine of divine simplicity? Briefly and most generally, it is the claim that in God there is no composition of any kind whatever. More particularly, and according to Aquinas,[19] there is in God no composition between material parts, none between form and matter, none between essence and existence, none between essence or nature and anything to which it might be ascribed, none between genus and difference, nor any between individual and properties. These are negative claims of which Maimonides would obviously have approved. Positively, however, the divine simplicity means that God is identical with his existence, his nature, and his real properties (though not with his Cambridge properties). Of all these claims the most basic is that of God's being identical with his existence, i.e. his being Subsistent Existence. From it all the others could be derived, and most importantly the identity between God and each of his attributes.

Not unexpectedly, the notion of a completely simple God has elicited widely diverse responses. Perhaps the most common is one of incredulity at the suggestion that his existence, knowledge, wisdom, power, and other attributes are all identical with God himself and, hence, with each other. Some have dismissed it as incoherent, adding that, even it were not, it would reduce God to the level of a property. How could his wisdom be the same as his mercy, or his mercy the same as his justice, or his intelligence the same as his power, and each of them the same as each other? How could those identities which are quite impossible in creatures be any the less impossible in God? Such critics describe the doctrine somewhat unflatteringly as guilty of 'sophistry and illusion,'[20] as 'flouting the most fundamental claims of theism,'[21] as unable to be construed 'in such a way that it fails to come out as necessarily false,'[22] and as failing to 'escape from a devastating atheological argument.'[23]

A second kind of response, and one endorsed by Brian Davies, attempts to divert such harsh criticisms by interpreting talk of divine simplicity as 'a piece of negative or apophatic theology and not a purported description of

19. *Summa Theologica*, I, 3.
20. A. Kenny, *Aquinas* (Oxford: Oxford University Press, 1980), 60.
21. A. Plantinga, *Does God Have a Nature?* (Milwaukee: Marquette University Press, 1980), 54.
22. C. Hughes, *On a Complex Theory of a Simple God* (Ithaca: Cornell University Press, 1989), 5.
23. R. Gale, *On the Nature and Existence of God* (Cambridge: Cambridge University Press, 1991), 29.

God. . . . its aim is to tell us the set of conclusions about God which are *not* to be drawn. And one thing being said by it is that God is not to be thought of (cannot be known) as something with properties distinguishable from each other, or as something we can conceive of as distinct from the nature we ascribe to it.'[24] Keith Ward, too, denies that the doctrine of the divine simplicity 'tells us anything positive about God at all.'[25] Thus interpreted, however, the doctrine would be rendered quite innocuous, since it would avoid saying anything about what God is, while saying a great deal about what he is not. But this, I shall be arguing, is effectively to eviscerate the doctrine, which admittedly has implications for what God is not, but only because it has something significant to say about what he is.

My own response is to rebut the criticisms not by interpreting the simplicity doctrine's claims negatively, but by showing that, when the identity claims are understood to be between limit cases rather than between limits simpliciter, they can not only be interpreted positively but are proof against the incredulity and perplexity which the doctrine has so often evoked. I mention the following merely as an advance sample of how some of the otherwise baffling identity claims are to be understood in terms of limit cases:

1.08.   'God is his existence' is to be understood as: 'The limit case instance of an individual = the limit case instance of existence.'

1.09.   'God is identical with his *F*-ness' is to be understood as: 'The limit case instance of an individual = the limit case instance of *F*-ness.'

1.10.   'God's *F*-ness is identical with his *G*-ness' is to be understood as: 'The limit case instance of *F*-ness = the limit case instance of *G*-ness.'

To explain and defend these and other identity claims, will be the work of later chapters from which it will emerge that claims, which would have been untenable had they been about *non*-limit cases, are in fact quite tenable when they are about *limit* cases.

Although it is important to explain how the divine simplicity itself is to be understood, it is perhaps the implications of that doctrine that will be the most telling in impressing upon us just how radical is the difference between

24. B. Davies, "The Doctrine of Divine Simplicity" in his (ed.) *Language, Meaning and God* (London: Geoffrey Chapman, 1987), 59 (my emphasis). Likewise, D. Burrell argues that to say that God is simple is 'a way of remarking that no articulated form of expression can succeed in stating anything about God' (D. Burrell, *Aquinas: God and Action* (London: Routledge & Kegan Paul, 1979), 18. Although Davies regards the simplicity doctrine as a piece of negative theology, he is not a negative theologian tout court. I say this because he does allow analogical predicates to be said of God, though for reasons that are quite independent of his views on divine simplicity. The same is true of Burrell.

25. Ward, *The Concept of God*, 158.

God and creatures, and what it means to say that his transcendence is nothing less than absolute. A quite basic difference is that, whereas creatures have abilities, capacities, and potentialities, a simple God has none whatever. It is not merely that all his abilities are never less than fully exercised, his capacities never less than fully extended, and his potentialities never less than fully actualized. Rather, it is that he has no ability to exercise, no capacity to extend, nor any potentiality to actualize. It is therefore a nonsense to regard him as having any ability or capacity to do or be *F*, no matter what *F* might be. Nor, of course, does it make any more sense to say that he had any *in*ability or *in*capacity to do or be *F*. The point is that the dichotomies ability/inability, capacity/incapacity, potentiality/nonpotentiality are no more appropriate to God than the dichotomy moral/immoral is to a raindrop. This means that we cannot say 'God can (or cannot) do or be *F*.' What we can and ought to say is, 'It can (or cannot) be that (God do or be *F*).' Unlike creatures, therefore, the only necessity or possibility applicable to God is not de re but de dicto.

Likewise, it makes no sense to say that a simple God can change: he is immutable, though not of course inactive. As for his power, he is unlike creatures in never exercising it *on* anything, and thus his activity is never anything but creative. This means that, in talk about his causation, the causal operator should always be used externally. For example, not 'God makes the Universe exist' but 'God makes it be that (the Universe exist),' not 'God acts on individual *X* to bring about *F*' but 'God brings it about that (*X* do *F*).'

At first sight, the emphasis on various aspects of God's otherness might seem to paint us into a corner since, in trying to say that God is so different from creatures as to be self-existent, identical with all his attributes, and not an individual, we find that the only language available to us is one that is applicable to things that are *not* self-existent, *not* identical with their attributes, and *are* individuals. Thus, we seem constrained to a silence, which could be broken only by retreating to the Anselmians' practice of attributing to God qualities that differ merely in degree from those had by humans. This difficulty would not arise if God-talk were restricted to saying about God something either merely negative, or merely relational, or both, e.g., if 'God is wise' were interpreted either as saying no more than 'God is not wise in the way that human beings are wise,' or as 'God is the cause of wisdom in creatures,' or both.[26] Nor would there be any difficulty if all God-talk were either

26. Although the few examples that I have given of God-talk are all predications — indeed, they are all predications employing *first*-level predicates — I use them not to suggest that all God-talk must be of this very basic kind, but simply because a grasp of more complex kinds of propositions presupposes a grasp of some atomic propositions, namely, those that enter into what Dummett calls the 'constructional history' of a proposition.

metaphorical or symbolic. It arises only for a God-talk which claims to be not only positive and often non-relational, but to be taken literally as well.

Although the problem would admittedly arise if the similarity in meaning between God-talk and creature-talk were one of univocity, it has been argued that there would be no problem at all if the similarity were less than univocity, i.e. if it were one of analogy. Opposing this move, however, critics are apt to maintain that if, for example, the predicates in 'Maria is intelligent' and 'God is intelligent' were to have any similarity of meaning at all, then there would have to be at least one respect in which the meaning of the predicate in the former was the same as that in the latter. But to admit even one respect in which they are the same would be to admit that they were univocal, and not analogical after all.

Although there is a ready reply to the last animadversion, an introductory chapter is no place in which to develop it. For the moment, suffice it to say that in chapter 8 I shall be arguing that the very simplicity doctrine that is alleged to preclude the use of God-talk in any positive and literal sense is, on the contrary, precisely the doctrine which also undergirds the analogical character of such God-talk. Moreover, it does so without detracting in any way from the divine transcendence.

The aforementioned consequences of God's being simple could have been expanded to include many others, notably in regard to the divine willing, the divine knowing, and the absence of any ability to choose in a God who is nevertheless free in regard to what he wills (other than his own goodness). Still, sufficient have been mentioned already to indicate why the simplicity doctrine is not merely some esoteric hypothesis of no practical significance, but is in fact quite central to our understanding of God's nature, his attributes, and the range of ways in which the absoluteness of his otherness is manifested. It is central, also, to an appreciation of the flaws that are endemic to perfect-being theology, negative theology, and process theology.

Before attending either to God's simplicity or to its distinctly arresting consequences, however, there is much to be done in chapters 2 and 3 in examining the role of existence as a real property of concrete individuals. An understanding of that role is a sine qua non for appreciating the much misunderstood, and hence much derided, notion of Subsistent Existence. And that, in turn, is basic to an appreciation of God's nature and simplicity.

Existence

To dispel the considerable misconceptions surrounding the notion of God as Subsistent Existence, there is a prior need to dispel the no less considerable misconceptions surrounding the rather more familiar notion upon which it depends.[1] I refer to the notion of existence as had by ordinary concrete individuals, about which three misconceptions are of particular concern:

A. The claim that '____ exists' is not a first-level predicable:[2] it is not predicable of concrete individuals. But if '____ exists' cannot be predicated of concrete individuals, it makes no sense to speak of their having existence as a property.

B. Moreover, even if (A) were false and '____ exists' were predicable of concrete individuals, existence would be no more than a Cambridge property:[3] it would not be a real one.

C. Even if (B) were false and existence were in fact a real property, it would be the most impoverished of real properties.

---

1. A not insubstantial part of this chapter has appeared earlier in my *From Existence to God* but is so basic to the present work that it needs to be repeated rather than merely referred to.

2. Following Geach, I say that an expression is a *predicable* if it *can* be attached to a subject, and a *predicate* only when it *is* so attached. Thus, in 'John lied in court' and in 'Whoever lies in court commits perjury' there are two occurrences of the one predicable, but only in the first case is it a predicate. The second case can be rendered as '$(x)(x$ lies in court $\supset x$ commits perjury),' in which '____ lies in court' is not predicated of anything. Cf. P. T. Geach, *Reference and Generality* (Ithaca: Cornell University Press, 3d ed., 1980), 50.

3. Geach has coined the term 'Cambridge change' to distinguish changes like butter's rising in price from real changes like butter's melting. I am simply extending the application of the adjective 'Cambridge' from changes to properties. Being at two dollars a kilo would be a Cambridge property of butter, whereas being melted (i.e., liquid) would be a real property.

Until all three claims about existence are rebutted, there would be little point in trying to defend the even more abstruse notion of Subsistent Existence. In the present chapter I shall respond to claim (A), leaving (B) and (C) to be answered in chapter 3.

Since it is only concrete individuals whose existence I want to discuss, it might be helpful to distinguish them immediately from individuals that are decidedly outside the scope of this chapter, viz., abstract individuals. Speaking generally, individuals are to be contrasted with universals, the mark of a universal being its instantiability (though not necessarily its being actually instantiated in anything), and the mark of an individual being the ability to instantiate universals together with the inability to be itself instantiated in anything. Individuals, however, may be concrete or abstract. They are concrete if they can either effect a real change, or be subject to a real change, or both; otherwise they are abstract.[4] I mention abstract individuals only to make it quite clear that neither they nor their existence is of any further interest for the purposes of this book. Indeed, all subsequent occurrences of the term 'individual' are to be understood as elliptical for 'concrete individual'.

I. '____ exists' is sometimes a First-Level Predicable

A feature of twentieth-century philosophy in the English-speaking world has been the widespread acceptance of the dictum 'Existence is not a predicate,' which were better expressed as '"____ exists" is not a first-level predicable,' i.e., '"____ exists" cannot be predicated of individuals.' In arguing *against* any first-level use for '____ exists,' proponents of the dictum have argued *for* its being always a second-level predicable.[5] My own view is that not all uses of '____ exists' are second-level ones, although the tenseless uses of '____ exists' and 'is' may be typically of this kind. There are, however, uses of '____ exists' and 'is' in temporal and modal contexts, many of which have to be admitted as first-level uses. I argue for these first-level uses as follows:

4. 'Abstract' has another and less common sense, though not one that I shall ever be using. As espoused by trope theorists, it is a sense according to whom an abstract entity is one that is 'got before the mind by an act of abstraction' (K. Campbell, "The Metaphysic of Abstract Particulars," *Midwest Studies in Philosophy* 6 (1981): 478. 'Abstract*ed*' would have been the more appropriate and less ambiguous term for such entities.

5. Predicables may be of various levels, depending on whether the something of which they can be said are individuals or properties. If sayable of individuals, they are first-level predicables. If sayable of what a first-level predicable stands for (a first-level property), they are second-level predicables. Still higher-level predicables can be said of higher-level properties.

What can be predicated of a property or a kind (incomplete
entities) differs *absolutely* from what can be predicated of an
individual (a complete entity).
But '_____ exists' is predicated both of individuals and of kinds.
Therefore, '_____ exists' has two senses, one as predicated of
individuals, the other as predicated of kinds.

The first premiss assumes that properties and kinds are the referents of
incomplete expressions (predicables), and hence are incomplete entities. Immediately, some might object that they are the referents not of predicables
but of abstract nouns, and hence are complete entities, albeit abstract ones.
Although I disagree with this view, I need not contest it here for, if it were correct, '_____ exists' would be *always* a first-level predicable, being predicable of
abstract objects no less than of concrete ones. This result would in fact be to
my advantage for, without impeding any attempt to show that existence is a
real property of concrete individuals,[6] it would relieve me of the task of dis-
crediting the view that takes '_____ exists' to be always a second-level predicable. Since many would not accept that properties and kinds are the referents
of abstract nouns, it is to them that the present argument is addressed.

Although there are two ways in which a predicable might be conceived of
as being said both of kinds and of individuals, it is not difficult to show that
neither is tenable. One way would be for a second-level predicable to be said
of them both, the other for a first-level predicable to be said of them both. In
regard to the first alternative, we should be clear as to precisely what kind of
expression can be said of what the first-level predicable refers to (viz., a kind,
or Fregean concept). If we consider the proposition '$(\exists x)(x$ is $F)$,' the first level
predicable is '_____ is F.' The second-level predicate attached to it is, however,
not simply '$(\exists x)$', but '$(\exists x)(x$ _____).' If we now ask whether the second-level
predicate could equally well be attached not only to a first-level predicable
but to a proper name, it is clear that it could not. The bound variable, which
filled the gap in '_____ is F,' has nowhere to go when '_____ is F' is replaced by
a proper name. The expression that results from such a combination is therefore not even a closed sentence.[7] Nor does anything better come of the second

---

6. Incidentally, the argument for this conclusion is inapplicable to the question of
whether existence is a *real* property of *abstract* individuals. Consequently, if '_____ exists'
were to be predicable of concrete and abstract objects alike, and if its referent in the first
case were a real property, its referent in the second case could still be a Cambridge property. In such circumstances, it would be plausible to suggest that there were two senses of
the *first*-level predicable, rather than the conclusion for which I do argue, namely, that
there is one sense for the first-level predicable and another for the second-level one.

7. By a closed sentence I mean a sentence containing no *un*quantified variables.

alternative mentioned above. If '____ is F' and '____ is G' are two first-level predicables, then the result of combining them would be '(____ is G) is F' or '(____ is F) is G.' The gaps indicate that neither combination would be even a closed sentence. Thus, it follows that no predicable, whether of first-level or second-level, can be said *both* of individuals and of kinds. And that establishes the major premiss.

The minor premiss can be proved in two ways: by contrasting singular existential propositions with one kind of general existential proposition, or by contrasting two kinds of general existential proposition. As an example of a singular proposition in which '____ exists' is predicated of an individual, one might be tempted to suggest 'Socrates exists,' were it not for oft-voiced protests of its not being 'usable outside philosophy.'[8] Rather than resist that claim, therefore, the example I propose is one that unquestionably *is* usable outside philosophy, 'Socrates no longer exists.'[9] But now it might be claimed that this can be rendered as 'There is (or exists) such a person as Socrates, who no longer exists.' But, surely that is saying that Socrates both exists and does not exist, which is absurd. What the claim ignores is that the uses of 'is' and 'exists' are not of the same level: whereas the first is a second-level use, the second is first-level. Hence, the proposition cannot be accused of claiming, absurdly, that there both exists and does not exist such a person as Socrates. It is saying, rather, that there is such a person as Socrates, and that that person does not exist (any longer); and there is no absurdity about that.

Not only is 'There is such a person as Socrates, who no longer exists' not absurd in the sense of being self-contradictory, it is not even absurd in the sense of being paradoxical. It is true that, if 'Socrates no longer exists' predicates '____ does not exist' of Socrates, we seem bound to allow that a property (viz. non-existence) can be acquired when there is no subject to acquire it; and that does indeed have all the appearance of paradox. For the appearance to have any substance, however, non-existence would have to be a *real* property. It need not be paradoxical at all if non-existence is only a Cambridge property like that of something's rising in price, or being famous; and if anything is a Cambridge property, it would have to be non-existence. So, the objection lapses.

8. E.g., C. J. F. Williams, *What Is Existence?* (Oxford: Oxford University Press, 1981), 79.

9. It might be objected that this means simply 'Socrates is no longer alive'. However, if 'exists' were synonymous with 'is alive,' we should be entitled to say 'The original St. Paul's is no longer alive.'

Turning now to the second-level uses of '____ exists,' they are both numerous and noncontroversial. 'Men exist' is a case in point, for it may often be rendered as '$(\exists x)(x$ is a man),' thus showing it not to be about any individual but, rather, about the property[10] *being a man*; for it says that being a man is instantiated at least once. Hence, 'Socrates no longer exists' and 'Men exist' provide the evidence necessary for our minor premiss that '____ exists' is predicable both of individuals and of kinds; for the only way of eliminating the difference between them is to reparse 'Socrates' as some kind of predicable, various versions of which I have rebutted in the appendix to chapter 4 of *From Existence to God*.

There is, however, a second way of proving the minor premiss, and this even without recourse to any *singular* existential propositions. It can be done by showing that not even all general existential propositions are about kinds, but that some are about individuals, as is exemplified by the two occurrences of 'Elephants exist' below:

2.01.   'Elephants exist, but mermaids do not.'
2.02.   'Elephants exist, but dinosaurs do not.'

In (2.01), '____ exists' is being said of the property of being an elephant, not about individual elephants, whereas in (2.02) it is being said of individual elephants, not about the property of being an elephant.

The foregoing claim can readily be substantiated. Since, in (2.01), 'Elephants exist' is being contrasted with 'Mermaids do not,' the sense in which 'elephants' is being used will be the same as that in which 'mermaids' is being used. Now, 'Mermaids do not exist' makes sense only if it means that all predications of the form 'x is a mermaid' are false. And it cannot mean that any proper name which turns 'x is a mermaid' into a true statement will turn 'x does not exist' into a true one, the simple reason being that there are no non-fictional proper names available for substitution in 'x is a mermaid.' Hence, 'mermaids' is being used to refer to the property of being a mermaid, not to individual mermaids. Consequently, 'elephants' in the contrasting clause must refer to the property of being an elephant. One might try to escape that conclusion by suggesting that a fictional name might very well be substituted for 'x,' as of course it might. That, however, would do nothing to alter the

---

10. Throughout the book I use the term 'property' in the very broad sense of 'whatever is attributed to something by a predicate.' Whether the property is of first or of higher levels will depend on whether the corresponding predicate is of first or of higher levels.

conclusion, since fictional individuals are not concrete individuals any more than rocking horses are horses.[11] So, there are no grounds for saying that non-fictional proper names can be substituted in 'x is a mermaid,' and hence no grounds for saying that 'Mermaids do not exist' can be indifferently about kinds or about concrete individuals.

In (2.02), on the contrary, neither does 'elephants' refer to the property of being an elephant nor 'dinosaurs' to the property of being a dinosaur. If they did, the proposition would not only be false but the conjunction 'but' would be quite misleading since there would be no point of contrast between the first and second clauses. The only way to retain that contrast is for 'elephants' and 'dinosaurs' to refer to individuals. So, in (2.02), 'Elephants exist' is a general existential proposition that is about individuals, as contrasted with the same clause in (2.01) which is not about individual elephants but merely about the property of being an elephant.

Thus, the minor premiss—that '____ exists' is predicable of both kinds and of individuals—has been vindicated a second time. From it and the major it follows that '____ exists' has two senses, one as predicable of individuals, the other as predicable of kinds, and which have been called by Geach the *actuality* and *there-is* senses respectively.[12] The fallacy in the dictum 'Existence is not a predicate,' therefore, has been to admit only the there-is sense, while dismissing the actuality sense.

II. The Misconception Underlying Opposition to '____ exists' Ever Being a First-Level Predicable

Critics of the actuality sense of '____ exists' have suggested that to admit existence as a property of individuals is to be led inevitably into rank absurdity, while to admit '____ exists' as a first-level predicable is to become enmeshed in an insoluble paradox generated by negative existential propositions. The alleged absurdity has been illustrated by David Londey in inviting us to 'reflect on the absurdity of a sheep-farmer who daily inspected his flock with the aim of sorting the existing sheep from the non-existent ones—searching for

11. Notice that the argument adopts no position as to whether either fictional or empty proper names belong to the same logical category as names that are both non-fictional and non-empty. The point on which the argument rests is the tautological one that empty names have no bearer at all and that, whatever the referent of fictional names may be, it is certainly not a *concrete* individual.

12. P. T. Geach, "What Actually Exists," supplementary volume of *Proceedings of the Aristotelian Society* 43 (1968): 7–16, especially pp. 7–8.

the stigmata of existence.'[13] As for the paradox generated by negative existential propositions, it is said to arise in this way. If '____ exists' is a predicable, then its negation should be a predicable also. But if '____ does not exist' is a predicable, then in 'Socrates does not exist' it is predicated of Socrates. But it can be predicated of him only if he exists. And similarly for all negative existential propositions — paradoxically, if '____ does not exist' is to be predicated at all, it can be predicated only of what *does* exist.

Looking afresh at the putative paradoxes and absurdities said to be generated by accepting '____ exists' as a first-level predicable, we might note that they stem not from allowing existence to be a real property but from allowing *non*-existence to be a real one. Only by thinking that non-existence was some kind of real property would any sheep-farmer be led to the absurdity of inspecting his flock 'with the aim of sorting the existing sheep from the *non*-existent ones,' or would a horticulturist be led to 'examine several specimens of blue buttercup before concluding that . . . as a variety *blue buttercup* lacks existence.' Only if non-existence were a real property would it seem paradoxical that '____ does not exist' could be true of Socrates only after there was any Socrates for it to be true of. Only if non-existence were a real property could 'Socrates no longer exists' imply that Socrates had suffered some posthumous loss. Considered thus, therefore, it might seem strange that the blame has been laid on treating existence as a real property of individuals, when it should surely have been laid on treating non-existence as one. Why deny that existence is a real property, when it was necessary only to deny that non-existence was such a property?

Perhaps the answer lies in the mistaken belief that the two denials are inseparable, and so there could be no denying non-existence to be a real property of individuals without denying existence to be one also. After all, if properties are what predicables stand for, how could it be said that '____ exists' stood for a real property, but that '____ does not exist' does not? If we accept existence as a real property, are we not bound also to accept non-existence as one? Clearly, these suggestions rest on two assumptions that need now to be tested:

13. D. G. Londey, "Existence," *Philosophia Arhusiensis* 1 (1970): 3. In similar vein, Christopher Williams asks what he would have done had he been told that blue buttercups did not exist. 'Would I have felt obliged to examine several specimens of blue buttercup before concluding that none of them exist, that as a variety *blue buttercup* lacks existence?' Emphasis in the original. C. J. F. Williams, *Being, Identity, and Truth* (Oxford: Oxford University Press, 1992), 1.

2.03.   that 'Socrates does not exist' contains a negative existential predicate.
2.04.   that a negative existential predicate stands for a real property.

In regard to (2.03), although '_____ does not exist' is a grammatical predicate in 'Socrates does not exist,' it does not follow that it must also be a logical one. We need to recognize the possibility of construing the proposition as having the logical form of 'It is not the case that (Socrates exists).' In that case, what is predicated (though not asserted) of Socrates would be simply '_____ exists' (and not '_____ does not exist'); and what would be asserted is that it is not the case that Socrates exists. On such an analysis of singular negative existential propositions, '_____ does not exist' need not be recognized as a predicate at all, and therefore non-existence need not be recognized as a property of any kind, whether real or Cambridge.

The distinction being invoked is one between internal or predicate negation on the one hand and external or propositional negation on the other. The difference between them has sometimes been thought to be that 'Socrates (does not exist)' says something about an individual (Socrates), whereas 'It is not the case that (Socrates exists)' says something about a proposition, viz. that the proposition 'Socrates exists' is false.[14] In neither case, however, is anything said about a proposition. On the contrary, in both cases something is said about an individual, namely, Socrates; the cases differ only in *what* they say about him. The former says that non-existence is had by Socrates; the latter denies that existence is had by Socrates.[15]

The distinction between internal and external negation in this context has sometimes been dismissed as 'a distinction without a difference.' Consider, however, the example '*a* is not moral,' which may mean either of two things. It may mean that *a* has the property of being non-moral; alternatively, it may simply be denying that *a* has the property of being moral. Internal negation ['*a* (is not moral)'] is being used in the first case, but external negation ['It is not the case that (*a* is moral)'] in the second. If, therefore, the distinction between internal and external negation were one without a difference, those two renderings should mean the same. Yet, that is just what they do not mean; for the first is to be taken as '*a* is immoral,' but the second as the quite different '*a* is either immoral or amoral.' The distinction seems therefore to be a substantive one. Nor does the distinction's absence from the predicate calcu-

---

14. C. J. F. Williams, *What is Existence?* 124.
15. Of course, if it is denied that existence is had by Socrates, it will *follow* that the proposition 'Socrates exists' is false. That, however, no more entitles us to say that the implicans is *about* the implicandum than conversely.

lus count against this conclusion. Rather, it is merely evidence of one of the many ways in which that calculus fails to do justice to ordinary language

If the distinction is a substantive one, it is not a matter of indifference whether 'Socrates does not exist' is rendered as '(Socrates) does not exist' or as 'It is not the case that (Socrates exists).' Because it is the former but not the latter that gives rise to problems, the latter is clearly to be chosen. In that case, 'Socrates does not exist' would not contain '____ does not exist' as a logical predicate; and so we could recognize existence as a real property without the embarrassment of having also to recognize non-existence as real. One might have thought that even those who recognize only external negation (and deny any difference here between it and internal negation) would be attracted to this conclusion.

There is, nevertheless, a further objection that might be raised for, even if '____ does not exist' has no logical role in 'Socrates does not exist,' it must surely be admitted that 'It is not the case that ____ exists' does have such a role, and that it is indeed a negative predicate. Since it is a negative predicate, and since properties are what predicates stand for, does not this mean that, wriggle as we might, we are unavoidably committed to the occurrence of some negative existential property? If so, the escape from the absurdities and paradoxes may have proved to have been entirely illusory.

It can of course hardly be denied that by removing the name 'Socrates' from 'It is not the case that (Socrates exists)' we obtain the negative predicable 'It is not the case that ____ exists.' However, it should be clear that the property for which it stands cannot be a real one. Why? Because that predicable has no part in the constructional history of 'It is not the case that (Socrates exists).' Consequently, any property of non-existence that 'it is not the case that ____ exists' might stand for could not be a real one, but only a Cambridge one. Now, paradox could not arise simply from non-existence being a property, but only from its being either a real property or being among such Cambridge properties (if any) whose acquisition is conditional upon their subject of attribution existing at that time. Since non-existence is a Cambridge property that requires no such precondition, it belongs to neither class; and hence its attribution to a deceased Socrates generates no paradox whatever. So much for considering 'Socrates does not exist' as being negated externally.

For good measure, the paradox can be shown not to arise even if the negation in 'Socrates does not exist' were to be *internal* rather than external. Of course, it is true that a predicable can be obtained by removing 'Socrates' from the proposition, though this time it will not be 'it is not the case that

____ exists,' but simply '____ does not exist.' The question is whether it stands for a real rather than a Cambridge property; and the first thing is to decide whether it forms part of the sentence's constructional history, which is as follows:

2.05.   Remove the proper name from an arbitrary sentence, 'Caesar exists,' to obtain the predicable '____ exists.'

2.06.   Negate this predicable to form '____ does not exist.'

2.07.   Insert 'Socrates' in the gap in '____ does not exist' to form '(Socrates) (does not exist).'

Since '____ does not exist' *does* form part of this constructional history, we have as yet no licence to preclude the property for which it stands from being a real one.

To settle that question, we need some criterion for deciding when individual *a* could lack some real property *F* only by having another real property non-*F* correlative to the one it lacks. Well, let us consider this not in regard to existence but in regard to the property red. The question is whether the absence of redness from something which could be red must bespeak the presence of a real property correlative to red. Certainly, if *a* were a piece of wood then it could lack redness only if it had some colour or colours other than red — be it brown, cream, fawn, or whatever — none of which could be dismissed as mere Cambridge properties. That does not settle the question, however, since the result would be very different if *a* were not a piece of wood but a piece of glass.

Now, although glass is like wood in being something that *could* be red, it is also unlike wood in that its failure to be red does not mean that it is any colour at all: it may be quite colourless. To say that it is non-red, therefore, is not to say that it has any *correlative* property, or at least not any that is real. It might of course be said to have the property of being non-coloured; but, then, so too might a pain or a flash of insight, though their being non-coloured could hardly be claimed as a real, rather than a Cambridge, property. Reflecting on this example, it is not difficult to see that lack of a real property *F* bespeaks the presence of a correlative *real* property non-*F* only if *F* and non-*F* are differentiae of the one generic property, or determinates of the one determinable. Thus, if red and non-red were related either as differentiae or as determinates of the property of being coloured, red could be lacking in an *a* that was coloured only if *a* had some colour other than red.

The relevance to the discussion of non-existence is fairly clear. If lack of existence in *a* (which had existed) were to bespeak the presence in *a* of non-existence as a real rather than as a Cambridge property, existence and non-existence should be related to some real property just as red and non-red would have had to be related to the real property of being coloured. For convenience, let us call this generic or determinable property 'E.' Then, just as red and non-red would have had to be understood as *coloured* red and *coloured* other than red, so existence and non-existence would have to be understood as being E in an existential way and being E in a non-existential way. Thus, whether a existed or did not exist, it would have some form of being: it would be E. But there is simply no such form of being. Hence, even if 'Socrates does not exist' were to contain the predicate '____ does not exist,' the property stood for by that predicate would be no more than a Cambridge one. Consequently, no paradox could arise from 'Socrates does not exist.' This had already been demonstrated for the case where the negation was taken to be external to the proposition; it has now been demonstrated for internal negation as well.

To sum up what I have been saying so far in this section. I have been arguing that there is no truth in the long-standing belief which denies that 'Socrates no longer exists' contains '____ exists' as a first-level predicate. That denial is made on the grounds that, if '____ exists' really were a first-level predicate, there could be no denying that 'Socrates no longer exists' contains a negative existential predicate, either '____ does not exist' or 'it is no longer the case that ____ exists.' In either case, so it is claimed, there would be no escaping the paradoxes and absurdities of existence. Such a view employs three main premises, the first two of which are quite explicit, but the third merely implicit, viz.,

2.08. that predicables are formed by removing a proper name from a proposition,

2.09. that predicables stand for properties,

2.10. that any negative existential property would have to be either a *real* one, or, if a Cambridge property, it must be one whose acquisition is conditional upon its subject of attribution existing at that time.

I accept (2.08); and I accept (2.09) as well. What I do not accept is the unspoken assumption expressed by (2.10). As I have shown, (2.10) is not true of the property stood for by the predicable 'it is not the case that ____ exists.' The same point holds even when the negation is taken to be internal, and the predicable is '____ does not exist,' for there, too, the relevant property is a Cambridge one. Thus, *no matter whether the distinction between internal and external negation in this context be accepted or rejected, the result is the same.*

In neither case are we committed to Socrates acquiring any property, real or Cambridge, whose acquisition is conditional upon his existing at that time. In neither case, therefore, does 'Socrates does not exist' generate the paradoxes or absurdities which would make it impossible to count '____ exists' as a first-level predicable. There is indeed no such impossibility.

In arguing for this conclusion, I have been responding to the challenge to produce a sentence which can be recognized as usable outside philosophy and which is formed by wrapping '____ exists' round a genuine proper name. If I have argued correctly, such propositions as 'Socrates no longer exists,' 'Socrates came to exist,' and 'Socrates ceased to exist' are among the various quite straightforward examples that fill the bill. For one thing, their use of '____ exists' as a first-level predicate has none of the unacceptable consequences alleged by Williams and many others. For another thing, they are undoubtedly 'usable outside philosophy.'

III. Conclusion

Based on the premiss that what can be predicated of an individual differs absolutely from what can be predicated of a kind, I have argued that there is indeed a first-level use of '____ exists.' The rationale for denying that use stemmed largely from the paradoxes and absurdities that such a position was alleged to generate. These, however, were readily resolved by exposing the falsity of their tacit assumption that existence could not be a real first-level property without non-existence likewise being a real property. There has, of course, been a spate of alternative proposals, ranging from the plausible to the contrived, some for treating '____ exists' as a second-level predicable and some for reducing it to various other first-level predicables of a non-existential kind, whether formal or otherwise. For replies to such proposals I refer the reader again to the appendix to chapter 4 of my *From Existence to God*.

From the fact that '____ exists' is a first-level predicable, it follows immediately that existence is a first-level property, a property of concrete individuals. As yet, however, there are no grounds for saying it is a real property rather than a Cambridge one, and still less for saying that it is a rich property. Arguments for both those claims will be provided in the following chapter as a necessary prelude to spelling out the notion of Subsistent Existence.

The Reality and Wealth
of Existence

It is worth recalling from the previous chapter that neither Londey nor Williams would have been in the least disquieted by the prospect of existence being merely a Cambridge property. What attracted their ridicule was the possibility of its being a real property, for that immediately evoked hilarious visions of sheep farmers 'searching for the stigmata of existence,' and of people being obliged 'to examine several specimens of blue buttercup before concluding that there were none.'

Their disquiet, however, would have been only partly allayed by being shown that the dreaded absurdities ensued only if *non*-existence were a real property. I say this because, once the putative absurdities could no longer be appealed to, there would be no reason to deny that '____ exists' was a first-level predicate and hence existence a first-level property. The issue then becomes what kind of first-level property existence is — Cambridge or real. One possible response is to argue that, if Socrates' existence were indeed a real property, it should be like his wisdom and other real properties. Since we can say what his wisdom 'adds' to him, we should therefore be no less able to say what his existence 'adds' to him. But that is just what we cannot do, for an answer to 'What does Socrates' existence add to him?' seems to be tantalisingly elusive. Surely, therefore, Socrates' existence can be no more than a Cambridge property, never a real one.

This is precisely the view with which I shall be taking issue, and shall be arguing that the question is unanswerable not because existence is merely a Cambridge property but because the question itself makes very dubious sense. Rather, it betrays a radical misunderstanding of just how Socrates is related to his existence. In fact, it assumes precisely what it purports to be proving, for it could not even be asked except by already tacitly assuming that existence was *not* a real property.

So, just how is Socrates related to his existence? Since we know how he is related to real properties like his wisdom, it is easy to assume that the relation to his existence would be no different. This is rather a non sequitur, however, for in the broad sense in which I am using the term, a property is simply whatever can be attributed to something by a predicate; and a *first*-level property is whatever can be attributed to an *individual* by a predicate. To say that Socrates' existence and his wisdom are both properties is therefore to say merely that each of them can be attributed to him by a predicate, which in the first case would be '____ exists' and in the second '____ is wise.' From this, however, it does not follow that each property is related to Socrates in the same way. Not only does it not follow but, as we shall see, it is not even true. And therein will lie the ground for maintaining that the ontological richness of Socrates' existing is to be ascribed primarily to his existence.[1] Indeed, it is this conclusion which in chapter 5 will underpin one of the main claims of this book, namely, that Subsistent Existence has all the attributes commonly associated with the personal God of classical theism.

The Relation of Socrates to His Existence

As a prelude to exposing how Socrates' existence and his wisdom differ qua properties, I should make it clear that, in my view, they are not properties *tout court*, but are instances of properties. Although wisdom as such, courage as such, understanding as such, existence as such, and so on can readily be conceived of (but not imagined), there are no entities corresponding to those conceptions: there are only *instances* of wisdom, courage, and so on. Socrates' wisdom, Aristotle's, and Plato's are each distinct instances of wisdom.

Instances of real properties are indeed entities — though only of a sort. Furthermore, since they are subject to change, they are concrete entities, not abstract. All the same, they are only *incomplete* entities, where 'incomplete' is to be understood in a Fregean sense.[2] That is to say, they are not individuated in their own right, but merely in virtue of something that *is* individuated in its own right (Socrates). Moreover, Socrates' instance of wisdom can occur only in him: if it doesn't exist in him, it doesn't exist at all. In recognizing such property instances, I differ sharply not only from those who think there are

1. Socrates' *existence* has always to be distinguished from Socrates' existi*ng*, Socrates' wisdom from Socrates' being wise, and similarly for his other properties. Socrates' existence and Socrates' wisdom are simply the instances of existence and of wisdom which are had by Socrates in Socrates' existing and Socrates' being wise respectively.

2. My argument for predicate instances as incomplete entities is given in part II of the appendix to this chapter.

no such entities—not even incomplete ones—but also from trope theorists who do think that there are such entities, but regard them as *complete* entities (tropes), little substances.[3] They would not be individuated by anything else, but would exist irrespective of whether they belonged to something or to nothing whatever. Elsewhere, however, I have argued that, by committing the cardinal sin of implying that the uninstantiable can in fact be instantiated, trope theory forfeits any claim to tenability. To be more exact, the individuals of trope theory can be shown to be instantiable in other individuals.[4]

Inherence of Properties: Existence vs. Wisdom

With the introduction of the notion of property instances, we can begin to explore the relations between Socrates and his instance of existence to determine whether any sense can be made of the notion of his existence *adding* anything to him. The strategy will be to compare it with his wisdom, about which two important, albeit obvious, points can be made. One is that Socrates' wisdom is distinct from Plato's and Aristotle's precisely in being the wisdom-of-Socrates rather than the wisdom-of-Plato or the wisdom-of-Aristotle. That is to say, its individuation is parasitic upon that of Socrates, rather than vice versa. This is what is meant by Socrates being logically prior to his wisdom in respect of *individuation*. The second point is that Socrates' instance of wisdom exists only to the extent that Socrates exists, only to the extent that it belongs to Socrates. That is to say, its actuality also is parasitic on that of Socrates. This is what is meant by Socrates being logically prior to his wisdom in respect of *actuality*. About Socrates' wisdom, therefore, we can say that Socrates is logically prior to it in two respects—in respect both of actuality and of individuation.

At this stage I should mention several points of terminology associated with the foregoing claims that I shall be employing in the following pages. In virtue of Socrates' wisdom being parasitic upon Socrates in respect of individuation, I shall call Socrates the 'individuator' of his wisdom. And in virtue of Socrates' wisdom being parasitic on him in respect of actuality, I shall call him the 'subject' in which his wisdom 'inheres.' Although 'subject' and

---

3. This theory has been proposed by G. F. Stout, *Studies in Philosophy and Psychology* (London: Macmillan, 1930); D. C. Williams, "On the Elements of Being," *Review of Metaphysics* 7 (1943–44): 1–18 and 171–92; K. Campbell, "The Metaphysic of Abstract Individuals," *Midwest Studies in Philosophy* 6 (1981): 477–88, and *Abstract Particulars* (Oxford: Blackwell, 1990).

4. The argument for this claim is to be found in my "Individuals and Individuality," *Grazer Philosophische Studien* 37 (1990): 75–91.

'inheres' are Aristotelian terms, I intend them to be understood solely in the sense outlined in the previous paragraph. If that corresponds to Aristotle's sense, well and good; if not, it is of no consequence so far as this book is concerned.

Just as there were two points to be made about Socrates' wisdom, so there are two to be made about his existence. One is that it is distinct from all other instances of existence precisely in being the existence-of-Socrates. That is to say, its individuation is parasitic on that of Socrates. For this reason Socrates is said to be logically prior to his existence in respect of individuation. In respect of individuation, therefore, Socrates' existence differs not at all from his wisdom. The question is whether the same can be said of it in respect of actuality. This therefore amounts to asking whether Socrates' existence is like his wisdom in having Socrates as a subject of inherence.

Now, it would make no sense to speak of a property inhering in a subject, unless there were a subject in which to inhere—unless the subject had some actuality at least logically prior to the property's inhering in it. Hence, Socrates' existence could not inhere in him unless there were a sense in which he himself was real logically prior to his existence. The suggestion that there is such a sense is in fact not without support, for it has sometimes been thought, and even thought to be self-evident, that Socrates could not have come to exist unless, prior to his existing, it was *possible* that *he* exist. Of course, since this is a de re claim, it could be true only if there were some *res* to which the possibility, potentiality, or capacity for existence could be ascribed.

Since it would make no sense to ascribe a potentiality or capacity to Socrates, if there were no Socrates in any world to be a subject of that ascription, the de re claim could be true only if there were some sense in which, even before his conception, it could have been said that *there was* a Socrates who was merely *able* to become actual. Since Socrates was not actual at that time, the 'is' would obviously have to be understood in a sense other than 'is actual.' And that means there would have to be a Socrates, though not one that *is* actual, only one that *could* be actual. Such an entity might thus be said to be merely a *possible* Socrates, though a real entity nevertheless. If there were such an entity, it might provide the subject in which Socrates' existence would inhere.

However much our robust sense of reality might rebel against a proposal of this kind, it is one that has enjoyed some currency, being described disapprovingly by Quine as 'the view that concrete individuals are of two kinds: those that are actualized and those which are possible but not actualized. Cerberus is of the latter kind, according to this view; so that there *is* such a thing as Cerberus, and the proper content of the vulgar denial of Cerberus is more correctly expressed in the fashion "Cerberus is not actualized".'[5]

A more sophisticated version of this view has been proposed by Alvin Plantinga. Although he allows that 'Hamlet and Lear do not in fact exist; but clearly they could have,' he denies that there is now any possible Hamlet or Lear to which the possibility of existing might be ascribed.[6] What do now exist, and to which possibilities are even now ascribable, are two individual essences (haecceities), each of which could become actual by being exemplified in a future Hamlet and Lear respectively. Until now, and maybe forevermore, these haecceities remain unexemplified. Thus, while neither Hamlet nor Lear can now be referred to, their haecceities can be both referred to and conceived of. Moreover, because the haecceities are now conceivable, there is a real sense in which the individuals that would exemplify them are also conceivable even before they come to exist.

Views like the foregoing seem to presuppose that the sole difference between existing individuals and future individuals is that the former *are* actual, whereas the latter merely *could* be actual. If the distinction they draw between existing and being actual were accepted, a future individual, or at least its individual essence (Socrateity), might be said to *exist* without ever having become *actual*. Moreover, that same individual essence, which now merely exists, *could* be actualized or incarnated in real life. I have mentioned these views because, if they were tenable, that would put an end to our enquiry about whether Socrates' existence was like his wisdom in having a subject in which to inhere. The answer would be an unmistakable yes.

To preclude any such answer, it is therefore important to recognize that these proposals are decidedly not tenable. As for the position to which Quine referred, I have argued in the appendix to this chapter that, before Socrates existed, he was not even conceivable let alone real in any sense at all. As for Plantinga's haecceities, I have argued that there can be no such entities. These haecceities have been saddled with a condition which it is impossible to satisfy, for they are required to be exemplifiable in no individual but the one, if any, in which they do happen to be exemplified. The claim is that, even before

---

5. W. V. Quine, *Methods of Logic* (London: Routledge & Kegan Paul, 3 ed., 1974), 214.

6. A. Plantinga, *The Nature of Existence* (Oxford: Oxford University Press, 1974), 214. For more on his haecceity theory, see his "Actualism and Possible," *Theoria* 42 (1976): 139–60; "On Existentialism," *Philosophical Studies*, 44 (1983): 1–20; "Reply to Kit Fine," in J. E. Tomberlin and P. van Inwagen eds., *Alvin Plantinga* (Dordrecht: Reidel, 1985), 329–49.

Socrates existed, there was an abstract entity (Socrateity) which could not be exemplified in any individual but Socrates. On the contrary, however, it would be an enormous fluke for Socrateity to be exemplified in any *human* individual at all, let alone in Socrates. As I have argued, it could equally have been exemplified in a grain of sand, or a rhinoceros, or even a poached egg.[7] The failure of the haecceitist proposal simply confirms the argument in this chapter's appendix for saying that no individuals are even conceivable at that time.[8]

To avoid any possible misunderstanding of that claim, however, I should make clear what it does *not* deny. It does not deny that even now descriptions are conceivable which fit no individual that has ever existed but which may well turn out to be a perfect fit for some individual in another thousand years or more. Hence, my claim is *not* that no description could ever be uniquely satisfied by a future individual, for of course it is possible, albeit highly improbable, that I now describe my niece to be born in two years, the last current model Mercedes to come off the assembly line in three years from now, and the island to emerge from the Atlantic ocean in fifty years, and describe them no less successfully than a niece born last year, a Mercedes now in the showroom, or the island of St. Helena.

Nor do I deny that quite detailed predictions may be formulated which no existing individual satisfies, but which may indeed be satisfied perfectly by an individual that has yet to exist. It may be tempting, and even natural, to construe these admissions as tantamount to accepting the conceivability of future individuals. In effect, I have been arguing that the temptation is to be

7. A detailed refutation of Plantinga's haecceitism occurs in my *From Existence to God* (London: Routledge, 1992), 51–60, and in "Future Individuals and Haecceitism," *Review of Metaphysics* 45 (1991–92): 2–28.

8. In addition to the counter-proposals that I have discussed, perhaps I should offer a brief word on the views of Nathan Salmon and David Kaplan which I have been charged with neglecting. As for Salmon, his suggestion that reference is possible to individuals that never exist is one that is irrelevant to the point that I have been defending, for I have been explicitly concerned solely with concrete individuals. Whatever individuals that never exist may be, they are certainly not concrete. Concrete individuals and individuals that never exist are no more two kinds of individual than positive growth and negative growth are two kinds of economic growth. As for Kaplan, one of his main concerns is with certain terms which 'refer directly without the mediation of Fregean *Sinn* as meaning.' In so far as his position concerns reference to present or past concrete individuals, it too is irrelevant to my conclusions. In so far as it also embraces reference to *future* individuals, it would be relevant but ineffectual, unless perhaps one wanted to deny—as I do not—that proper names are rigid designators.

given short shrift, and that 'Tom satisfies description D' does not warrant the conclusion 'Tom was conceived of in description D,' nor does 'Tom satisfies prediction P' warrant the conclusion 'Tom was conceived of in prediction P.' Even if an individual could have been exhaustively *described* before it existed, the description could equally have been satisfied not just by the individual that did satisfy it but by any number of clones. The propositions employing the description may indeed be *made true* by some future individual. It is false, however, that they are *about* any future individual.[9]

Individuation without Inherence

The failure of attempts to provide some sense in which Socrates would be real even before he existed simply confirms the earlier conclusion that Socrates really is logically posterior to his existence in respect of *actuality*. Such logical posteriority has therefore to be reconciled with Socrates' logical priority to his existence in respect of *individuation*. Unless one were some kind of trope theorist, one might have thought there was no way in which Socrates' existence could be individuated except by its inhering in Socrates. The fact of its not inhering in anything should therefore undermine any claim to his existence being a real property like his wisdom, and suggest that it could be no more than a Cambridge one. Before accepting that inference, however, we might be wise to reconsider whether properties can be individuated only by *inhering* in an individuator. Perhaps there is more than one way of Socrates' being an individuator, more than one relation to Socrates in virtue of which a property instance might be distinguished from all others.

To develop this suggestion, consider the unlikely analogy of water in a bucket. Obviously, the bucket separates one mass of water from all others, and for that reason might unwittingly be regarded as individuating its contents. But now suppose we freeze the water and remove the bucket from around it. The fact that it still remains distinct from all other masses of water shows that the bucket is certainly not its individuator but merely its container or recipient. It is no more an individuator than a knife is the individuator of

9. To paraphrase Gilbert Ryle, the prediction of the birth of a son to the man and woman who came later to generate Socrates could, in principle, be as specific as you please. But one thing the forecaster could not do—logically and not merely epistemologically could not do. In his prediction he could not use with their normal force the term 'Socrates' or the pronoun 'he.' G. Ryle, *Dilemmas* (Cambridge: Cambridge University Press, 1954), 54. A. N. Prior makes the same point in "Identifiable Individuals" in his *Papers on Time and Tense* (Oxford: Oxford University Press, 1968), 72.

the one kilo of butter that it cuts from a ten kilo block. Although the kilo does indeed *become* an individual in virtue of the knife's activity, its actually *being* an individual is quite independent of the knife: it is in fact an individual in its own right. What therefore delineates the individual masses of butter and of water from each other and from all other individuals, is obviously not some subject in which they inhere or are received, but simply their own bounding surface. Without at least some bounding surface, they would not be individuated at all, but simply subsumed in larger masses of butter and water. This would be so, even if they were infinitely large.

Although neither the water nor the butter are properties, their individuation may nevertheless have some implications even for the individuation of Socrates' existence. What is of particular interest for our purposes are the interrelations between them and their bounds.[10] In respect of *individuation* the bound is logically prior to the water and the butter: it is in virtue of being bounded that they are distinct from all other individuals. In respect of *actuality*, however, the bound is logically posterior to what it bounds: it is in virtue of the water and butter that their bounds are actual, and not vice versa. Here, therefore, is what we had been seeking — one possible conception of individuation in which the individuator is not logically prior, in respect of actuality, to what it individuates.[11] What the example suggests is that there should be no difficulty about accepting Socrates' existence as a *real* property, despite Socrates not being a subject in which it inheres; for he could still individuate his existence provided he were not its subject but, in some sense, its bound.

Can we be more specific about the sense in which Socrates bounds his existence? We can, if we bear in mind that the ways in which existence might be manifested are extraordinarily wide-ranging, and no one individual comes even close to manifesting them all. The sense in which Socrates bounds his existence is in limiting these ways to those that find their manifestation in him: an instance of existence that is bounded by Socrates is one from which

10. For the scientifically minded, I should explain that I am not using 'bound' in the sense in which a cricket ball would be said to have *no* bound (because having no edge). Rather, I am using it in the straightforward non-scientific sense in which a cricket ball would indeed be bounded (because having a boundary surface).

11. Two points about the examples I have chosen. The first is that their value relies not on the conception of the bounds of the water and butter having to be correct but merely on their ability to alert us to a new way of viewing Socrates' relation to his existence. The second point is that the value of the examples would be in no way impugned by suggesting that perhaps some individuals are not spatially bounded at all.

all but the socratic ways of manifesting existence have been excluded.[12] The conception of Socrates and his existence which has at last emerged is therefore one that turns on its head the unreflective notion of his existence as *actualizing* him. On the contrary, the less misleading notion is of Socrates as *socratizing* his existence. However, let me recall that this is not Socrates' sole function for, in addition to socratizing his existence, he also individuates it, thereby distinguishing it from all other instances of existence — even from those that might be bounded by his *clones*.

As a caveat, I should add that to say that Socrates socratizes his existence is not to say that Socrates does anything to his existence. Socrates does not *impose* the limit or bound, but *is* that limit or bound. Not even God imposes the bound. True, he is its contractor or constrictor, but that means merely that he brings it about that (existence occurs as contracted to the ways in which it is manifested by Socrates). It does not mean that there is any such entity as existence tout court on which he acts to contract it.

Immediately, it might be objected that this conclusion is altogether too slick, and relies on an analogy that limps rather badly. Of course, every analogy limps, otherwise it would not be an analogy. The objection here, however, seems to be that the water and butter analogy limps precisely because it relies on there being some larger mass of water and of butter from which the bucket and knife detach the appropriate portions. If so, it would offer no parallel at all with Socrates' existence, for there is simply no 'mass' of existence from which a portion could be detached for Socrates. Nor is there even such an entity as existence tout court floating around in any platonic heaven.

Although these dissimilarities are undeniable, they do nothing to detract from the utility of the analogy, for they are relevant only to the *process* by which there come to be distinct portions of water and butter, but quite irrele-

---

12. Although some mediaeval writers spoke of Socrates as 'contracting' or 'determining' his existence, it is doubtful whether they regarded him as *bounding* it. Aquinas, for example, speaks of the existence of a created form as being 'received and contracted to a determinate nature' ('receptum et contractum ad determinatam naturam.' *Summa Theologica*, I, 7, 2c). Even more interesting is: 'In everything that exists subsequent to the first being, . . . its existence is received in something that contracts it' (Omne igitur quod est post primum ens, . . . habet esse in aliquo receptum, per quod ipsum esse contrahitur.' *De Creaturis Spiritualibus*, 1c). This would seem to indicate that the contraction of existence would be a consequence of its being *received* in Socrates. If that is a correct interpretation, it would differ from my view of Socrates as bounding his existence rather than as receiving it. I have been insisting that a bound is not to be confused with a container or recipient (if any) that might impose a bound.

vant to the *product* of that process, which is a portion of water and a portion of butter each distinct from all other individuals. The crucial point in the analogy is that the individuation of those portions—their being distinct from all other concrete individuals—is manifested by their having distinct bounds.

Finally, it might be objected that the bounds mentioned in the analogy were merely spatial ones—surfaces—but there is far more to Socrates than the merely spatial. Indeed there is: there are intellectual, sensory, emotional, and biological areas, to mention but a few. Significantly, however, there was no time when Socrates' capacities in these areas were ever limitless. Moreover, the fact that the limits could expand and contract is no more evidence of the capacities having no limits at all than the fact that an individual's surface can expand and contract is evidence of its having no spatial limit—no surface at all. So, in saying that Socrates was the bound of his existence, I am not denying that the bound was multifaceted, nor am I suggesting that the bound is unchanging. The point of using the notion of a bound was to indicate the kind of relation which would allow Socrates to individuate his existence without, however, being its *subject* of inherence.

To repeat. We have been impelled to a radical revision of Socrates' role by the twin and prima-facie conflicting considerations of his being logically prior to his existence in respect of individuation, but logically posterior to it in respect of actuality. How could Socrates individuate his existence without its *inhering* in him? The conflict was resolved by recognizing that Socrates individuates his existence not by being its subject of inherence but by being its bound. It is precisely in being bound by Socrates that it is distinguished from Plato's instance of existence, from Aristotle's, and from every other instance of existence as well.

Socrates the Bound = Socrates the Individual

Now, however, it might be urged that, by conceiving of Socrates as a bound, we have surrendered all claim to his being an individual, a primary substance. Let me try to relieve that fear by noting that if Socrates is an individual, the relationship between him and his existence must be such as to underpin the following three claims:

3.01.   Socrates individuates his existence, rendering it not only non-instantiable but also distinct from every other instance of existence.

3.02.   '____ exists' can be predicated of Socrates.

3.03.   Socrates' existence is a property of him.

Provided these points are not threatened by his being a bound, there is no inconsistency in Socrates being also an individual, a primary substance.

As for the first point, he can truly be said to individuate his existence, because it is precisely qua bounded by Socrates—rather than by Plato or any other individual—that his instance of existence is both non-instantiable in anything and is distinct from all other instances of existence. And, even though the bound may undergo change in various ways over time, that individuation is never impugned since it is tautologically true that his existence never has any bound but him, no matter what changes he may undergo.

In regard to the second point, it has to be noted that, qua bounding his existence, Socrates is undoubtedly an actual bound rather than an imaginary one or a possible one. However, to say that he is actual when bounding his existence is to say that he exists. Hence there can be no objection to predicating '____ exists' of him in 'Socrates exists.' And if '____ exists' can be predicated of him, so also can various non-existential predicates like '____ is brown' and '____ is talking.'

As for the third point, initially it may seem odd to say that Socrates' existence is a property of Socrates, for how could what is bounded be a property of its own bound? This ought not be a problem once it is recalled that I am using the term 'property' in the very wide, though entirely legitimate, sense of 'whatever a predicate attributes to something.' Precisely because '____ exists' can be predicated of Socrates, and because his existence is what that predicate attributes to him, it is perfectly entitled to be called a property of him. Objection could be taken to this only if it were thought that his existence had to be like his non-existential properties not simply in being attributable to him by a first-level predicate but also in being related to him in the same way as are his non-existential properties. The broad notion of a property, however, no more entails that properties be related uniformly to their bearers than that they be uniformly real, or uniformly Cambridge, or uniformly formal, or uniformly non-formal, or uniformly of one level.

The last requirement is therefore like the first two in offering no obstacle to Socrates being the bound of his existence rather than its subject or recipient. Since all three requirements have been met, Socrates' role as the bound of his existence is quite consistent with his being an individual, a primary substance.

The Reality of Existence Revisited

Let me now return to the question, 'What does existence add to Socrates?' If this is not to be understood as tacitly assuming that existence is merely a

Cambridge property, it must be elliptical for, 'If his existence were a real property of Socrates, what would it add to him?' We have seen that his existence would be logically prior to him, and hence that he could not be a subject in which it inheres. But, in that case, it is simply not the kind of item that might be described as 'added' to him. So, the question of what it adds is a nonsense.

What, then, would the proper question be? Since existence has sometimes been spoken of as 'contracted' by Socrates, it may be tempting to think that the appropriate question is not what existence adds to Socrates but what Socrates subtracts from existence. But underlying this question is exactly the same misconception as the earlier one, for it too assumes that Socrates receives existence and, in doing so, contracts it. The truth, therefore, is that it makes no more sense to ask what Socrates subtracts from existence than it does to ask what existence adds to him.

The proper question is one which assumes nothing whatever about Socrates' role, and certainly not that he is a subject or recipient in which his existence would inhere. Rather, the question should be simply, 'What are the respective roles of Socrates and his existence in his existing?' The answer, as it has turned out, is that Socrates' role is that of a bound vis-à-vis his existence as what he bounds. To the further question of whether his existence is a real or a Cambridge element in Socrates' existing, the answer has to be that it is real. Socrates could hardly be both real and a bound, if what he bounds were not real also.

The Wealth of Existence

Because Socrates is the bound of his existence rather than its subject of inherence, it will prove to be a monumental misconception to accept Kenny's view of '___ exists' as the 'thinnest possible kind of predicate' and, by implication, existence as the thinnest or most impoverished of all properties. Such a view rests on a rather exiguous understanding of existence as simply 'that attribute which is common to mice and men, dust and angels.'[13] The modicum of truth in this claim is merely that, if a mouse, a man, a speck of dust, and an angel all exist, then what is common to them is that each has an instance of existence. From that, as we shall see below, it does not follow that there is no difference between those instances, and still less that they are impoverished.

13. A. Kenny, *The Five Ways* (London: Routledge and Kegan Paul, 1969), 92.

The Wealth of Existence

The claim that the existence of an individual is the most impoverished of properties can be challenged both negatively and positively. Negatively, I have done so already by noting that it presupposes a relation between Socrates and his existence that simply does not obtain, one in which Socrates would be the recipient or subject of his existence. Positively, it can be challenged by reflecting on the relation that does in fact obtain between them—that of bound to bounded. Obviously, the ontologically basic element in the bound/bounded relation is not the bound but what is bounded. Equally obviously, it is the bound that is ontologically parasitic. Accordingly, it is Socrates' existence that is ontologically basic, and Socrates that is parasitic upon it. On the view of Socrates as the recipient or subject of his existence or as having the potentiality to be actualized, it was possible (though not inevitable) that his existence be as impoverished or vacuous as Kenny has deemed it to be. Since, however, he is not the subject in which his existence inheres but merely its bound, there can hardly be any question of his existence being impoverished, since it is not in the bound that the ontological riches lie but in what is bounded.

A further consequence is that, even though every individual bounds an instance of existence, not every instance of existence will be equally rich. An amoeba will be a more constricting bound than a gazelle, which in turn will be more constricting than a human. And naturally there would be variations from one amoeba to another, from one gazelle to another, and from one human to another. Speaking generally, therefore, the richness of an instance of existence will vary in direct relation to the constricting character of its bound: an individual endowed with more exalted *kinds* of properties like intelligence, wisdom, benevolence will be a less constricting bound than one having less exalted kinds and, of two individuals having the same kinds of properties, the less constricting will be the one that has those properties to the higher degree. Thus, Kenny notwithstanding, the richness and complexity of any instance of existence does indeed vary relative to what it is the existence of.

A Corollary Concerning '____ exists'

I have dwelt at length on the error of conceiving the ontological role of existence as one of inhering in or of being received by an individual. We need also to advert to the correlative misconception concerning the logical role of '____ exists,' namely, of taking its role in 'Helen exists' to be the same as the vast number of predicates like '____ is brown' in 'Helen is brown' and 'This gazelle is brown.' The point about '____ is brown' is that it can attribute exactly the same kind of property to individuals as diverse as Helen, a gazelle, or even a plank of wood: the brownness had by each individual may differ neither in kind nor degree from that had by any other. To think of '____ exists' in this way would be to regard it as attributing to Helen neither more nor less than it does to a grain of sand. What this sadly ignores, however, is that by no means all predicates conform to the model of '____ is brown.' An everyday example of a quite different model is '____ is fast' in 'Simon (a snail) is fast,' 'Helen (a human) is fast,' 'Gerry (a gazelle) is fast,' and 'Fred (a fighter plane) is fast.'

The relevance of these four propositions is that sameness of predicate in each of them does not entail sameness of speed in each of their subjects. Rather than being the same for each subject, the property being fast is directly relative to whatever its subject may be. Similarly with '____ is big,' which can be said of a flea no less than of an elephant or a skyscraper without however attributing the same size to each. 'Fast' and 'big' are what Geach has called 'predicative' adjectives, one mark of which is that 'X is a fast snail' does not break up into 'X is fast' and 'X is a snail,' nor does 'X is a big flea' break up into 'X is big' and 'X is a flea.' On the other hand, 'X is a brown snail' does break up into 'X is brown' and 'X is a snail,' and 'X is an infectious flea' does break up into 'X is infectious' and 'X is a flea.' 'Brown' and 'infectious' are therefore not predicative adjectives but what Geach calls 'attributive' adjectives. Unlike 'fast' and 'big,' what they attribute is invariant as between humans, gazelles, or fighter planes, or anything else.

Since instances of existence vary in direct relation to the individuals that bound them, it is obvious that '____ exists' cannot be like '____ is brown' and '____ is infectious' but is in fact like '____ is fast' and '____ is big,' for which reason we might call it not a predicative adjective (for it is not an adjective at all), but a predicative term. One of Kenny's misconceptions was to treat it in effect as if it were like '____ is brown' and '____ is infectious,' an error which can hardly be dismissed as of little consequence, for it has spawned the view that '____ exists' is the thinnest of all predicates; and that is as far from the truth of the matter as it is possible to be.

The 'On/Off Character' of Existence

The foregoing conclusions concerning the wealth of existence and the logical status of '____ exists' as a predicative term are implicitly challenged by the deceptively plausible argument of Christopher Hughes in contesting the claim that 'different sorts of esses will be limited to varying extents by different sorts of forms,'[14] a view expressed by Aquinas in saying that 'a thing is more or less excellent according as its esse is limited to a greater or lesser special mode of excellence.'[15] Hughes' argument is simply this:

> Existence is an on/off property: 'either you're there or you're not.'
> Because existence is on/off, it would seem, either you have it according to its full power or you don't have it at all.

The inference being drawn is that because various electrons, amoebae, and humans all do exist, they all exist according to what Hughes calls 'the full power of existence.' Consequently, we are asked to accept that there is not even a difference of degree, let alone of kind, between the instances of existence had by any of these very diverse individuals.

Of course, there can be no denying the truth of such propositions as 'Either X exists or it does not' and 'Either Y exists or it does not'; and they might well warrant the view that existence is an on/off property. What they fail to warrant, however, is any leap to the conclusion that X's existence can be neither more nor less 'fully powered' than Y's, or that the instance of existence had by an electron could be neither more nor less rich than that had by Einstein. It fails precisely because it treats '____ exists' in 'X exists' and 'Y exists' as if it were an attributive term which it is not, rather than as the predicative term which it is. To treat it as a predicative term is to recognize that, just as an instance of the property of being fast varies relative to whether it is had by a fighter plane, a gazelle, or a snail, so do the instances of existence had by X and Y vary relative to whether the latter are electrons, amoebae, or humans. Consequently, although it may be true that existence is an on/off property, it is quite false that an instance of existence had by an electron can be neither more nor less rich than an instance had by Einstein: the difference is simply incalculable.

Illustrating the Bound/Bounded Relation

Before I conclude, it might be helpful to consider an analogy in order to illustrate, however imperfectly, the difference between conceiving of Socrates' existence as inhering in him and conceiving of it as being bounded or socratized by him. I should stress that the analogy is precisely that—an analogy.

14. C. Hughes, *On a Complex Theory of a Simple God* (Ithaca: Cornell University Press, 1989), 26.
15. *Summa contra Gentiles*, I, 28.

Any reader who finds it unhelpful or even a hindrance, should ignore it altogether.

Consider a light beam whose cross-section is not white at all but is entirely a pattern of different colours or mixtures of colours. Throughout the whole length of the beam—from its source and for as far as it shines—its cross-section exhibits this same colour pattern. In other words, at any point along the beam at which a white surface was interposed, it would reflect that same pattern of colours. Suppose, too, that the light source is such as to be able to generate a multitude of differently patterned beams but unable to generate any that are patternless (white), or any with more than one pattern. That is to say, the beams are either generated qua configured with just one pattern or they are not generated at all. I make this stipulation to preclude the pattern from being thought to be imposed on a beam that had already been generated, as might happen by passing white light through a patterned filter. Rather, the beam emerges from its source as a package, as configured with just one pattern.

The light source is proposed as a parallel for God, the pattern in the beam as a parallel for Socrates, the beam itself as a parallel for Socrates' existence, and the patterned beam as a parallel for Socrates' existing. If we now compare the patterned light beam with Socrates' existing, we find that they parallel each other in four respects:

3.04.　There can be no pattern except as the pattern of a beam.
　　　　There can be no Socrates except as the bound of his existence.
3.05.　There can be no light beam that is not patterned.
　　　　There can be no instance of existence that is not bounded.
3.06.　The generator does not act on anything external to it to produce the patterned beam.
　　　　God does not act on anything external to him to produce Socrates' existing.
3.07.　The generator is the sole cause of the patterned light beam.
　　　　God is the sole cause of Socrates' existing.

There are, however, at least three respects in which the analogy does break down. The first is that the generator expends energy in producing the patterned beam, whereas God expends no energy in producing his creatures. A second is that the light beam is itself not existence but merely has existence. A third disanalogy is that the patterns are individuated by the beam, whereas Socrates is not individuated by his existence but vice versa. We ought not be dismayed by such disanalogies since, if creation were simply on all fours with generating the light beam, the generator itself would be a creator. If an analogy were not defective in some respect, it would not be an analogy at all. In evaluating the present analogy, therefore, the issue is not whether it is free of disanalogies—for it never can be—but whether its point is at all enlightening despite those disanalogies.

The one and only point of the present analogy is to illustrate something of the difference between conceiving of Socrates as the subject in which his existence inheres and conceiving of him as the bound of his existence. The parallel to considering him as the subject of his existence would have been a painting on which white light shone from the generator to illuminate the painting's pattern of colours. Not only is the painting real before being illuminated, it also has the potentiality to be illuminated. Thus, it bears no resemblance to a Socrates who, in his own right, has neither actuality nor potentiality. The distinctive feature of the analogy that I have proposed is that the colour pattern has neither actuality nor potentiality in its own right but has them only to the extent that it is a feature of the light beam itself. It constitutes a constriction on the fullness of white light. In these particular respects it resembles Socrates, who also has neither actuality nor potentiality in his own right, and who is a constriction on the many ways in which existence can be manifested.

In the light-beam case, we find that the pattern is parasitic on the beam in respect of actuality. In the case of Socrates, he is parasitic on his existence in respect of actuality. We find too that the richness of the beam (the number, strength, and arrangement of frequencies) will vary from beam to beam, and that it will do so relative to variations in the patterns bounding the beams. Similarly, the richness of existence varies from instance to instance, and does so relative to the individual that bounds it. This, therefore, helps to illustrate why it would be mere pretence to accept that Socrates' instance of existence was ontologically prior to Socrates, while at the same time continuing to dismiss his existence either as the most impoverished of all properties, or even as being invariant across the whole range of individuals.

Conclusion

Opponents of the claim that Socrates' existence is a real property are apt to make great play of questions like, 'Just what is Socrates' existence, if it is not Socrates, nor any of his (non-existential) properties, whether relational or not? What difference does it make? Just what does it add to him?' The fact that the questions are unanswerable is mistaken for evidence that the criticisms are well-founded. Nothing could be further from the truth. No answer is forthcoming not because the criticisms are well-founded but because they are so desperately ill-founded, resting as they do on the false assumption that Socrates' existence could not be a real property unless it added something to him. And that particular mistake stems from the single-minded concentration on Socrates' existence as a property, and the correlative neglect of the relation that is peculiar to its being an *existential* property.

Central to our determining the peculiar character of Socrates' relation to his existence has been the recognition that he cannot be logically prior to his existence, and hence cannot be the subject in which his existence inheres. If Socrates really were something in which his existence inhered, then he would require some actuality in its own right, quite independently of his existence. Independently of his existence, however, Socrates has no actuality whatever, neither is he even conceivable. For just that reason, questions of his existence adding anything to him cannot arise—logically cannot arise.

The question which does arise and which Davies and others would have been entitled to ask is, how can Socrates possibly individuate his existence without being the subject in which it inheres? The answer is that he can do so by being its bound. This has ground-breaking consequences not only for the property existence but also for the predicate '____ exists.' *Firstly*, his existence can no longer be dismissed as so 'thin' or so 'impoverished' a property as to be virtually vacuous. It is, on the contrary, extraordinarily rich, since it is only in virtue of his existence that Socrates has such non-existential properties as he does have—a claim that is notably stronger than the true but trivial point that Socrates has his properties if and only if he exists. *Secondly*, existence can no longer be regarded as invariant from individual to individual. On the contrary, the richness of existence does vary markedly from individual to individual, and even more so from one kind of individual to another. Mutatis mutandis, what is true of instances of existence is equally true of instances of '____ exists,' the sense of which can no more be regarded as independent of its subject than are the senses of '____ is big' or '____ is fast.' The third consequence, therefore, is that '____ exists' is not an attributive term as it seems tacitly to have been regarded; rather, it is a predicative term.

These conclusions have complemented those in the preceding chapter that '____ exists' is a first-level predicate and existence a property of individuals, for they show just what distinguishes existence from all other properties—whether they be real or Cambridge, first-level or higher-level, formal or non-formal. The distinguishing mark is that existence is the only property to be related to an individual as to its bound. These conclusions will help to dispel some of the deep misconceptions to be exposed in subsequent chapters, and which underlie the attempt to dismiss Subsistent Existence as simply 'sophistry and illusion.'[16]

Appendix

I. Individuals Are Inconceivable before They Exist

The argument for the inconceivability thesis is simply this:

3.08.   No concrete individual could have been referred to before it existed.

3.09.   If no concrete individual could have been referred to before it existed, it could not have been conceived of before it existed.

3.10.   Therefore, no concrete individual could have been conceived of before it existed.

The argument for the second premiss is entirely straightforward. For an individual to be conceivable, it must be possible to say at least something about it: that of which literally nothing could even in principle be said, and about which literally no proposition could even in principle be formed, would be inconceivable. But nothing could be said, nor any proposition be formed, about anything to which no reference was possible.

The argument for the first premiss is rather less straightforward, but turns on the simple truth that, once a proposition like '"Socrates" refers to Socrates' was true at a given time a, nothing *thereafter* could prevent its having been true at that time. This, I should note, is sharply to be distinguished from the claim that '"Socrates" refers to Socrates' could not be true at one time but false at a later time. Although I think that it too is true, it plays no part whatever in the following argument:

3.11.   Had '"Socrates" refers to Socrates' ever been true at any time a before Socrates existed, it could *thereafter* never fail to have been true at time a.

3.12.   But, until Socrates did come to exist it was *always* possible that he not come to exist, and hence that '"Socrates" refers to Socrates' could never have been true at time a.

16. A. Kenny, *Aquinas* (Oxford: Oxford University Press, 1980), 60.

3.13. Therefore, it is not the case that '"Socrates' refers to Socrates' could have been true at any time *a* before Socrates existed.

In arguing for (3.11) and (3.12), it will be helpful to employ the following symbols:

> Let *p* be the proposition '"Socrates" refers to Socrates.'
> Let *a* be a time *before* Socrates came to exist.
> Let *b* be any time *after a* but *before* Socrates came to exist.
> Let 'T*ap*' be '*p* is true at time *a*.'
> Let M be the operator 'it is possible that.'

Argument for Premiss (3.11):

3.14. Suppose that '"Socrates" refers to Socrates' had in fact been true at time *a* before he came to exist in 470 B.C., i.e., T*ap*.
3.15. But, if that had been the case, then at time *b* it would have been no longer possible to prevent '"Socrates" refers to Socrates' from having been true at time *a*, i.e., *if* T*ap* then T*b*~M~T*ap*.
3.16. Therefore, at time *b* it would have been no longer possible to prevent '"Socrates" refers to Socrates' from having been true at time *a*, i.e., T*b*~M~T*ap*.
3.17. But (3.16) entails that at time *b* it would not have been true that '"Socrates" refers to Socrates' possibly be prevented from having been true at *a*, i.e., ~T*b*M~T*ap*.
3.18. Therefore, at time *b* it would not have been true that '"Socrates" refers to Socrates' possibly be prevented from having been true at *a*, i.e., ~T*b*M~T*ap*.

Argument for Premiss (3.12):

3.19. It is possible that the conditions at time *b* could have been such as to have prevented Socrates from ever coming to exist.
3.20. But, had Socrates never come to exist, he could never have been referred to.
3.21. Therefore, at time *b* it would have been possible that 'Socrates' never have referred to Socrates.
3.22. But, had 'Socrates' *never* referred to Socrates, '"Socrates" refers to Socrates' would not have been true at time *a*.

3.23.   Therefore, at time b it would have been true that '"Socrates' refers to Socrates' possibly be prevented from having been true at a, i.e., $TbM\sim Tap$, which contradicts (3.18).

In examining the argument's premises, it needs to be remembered that the necessity being employed is not logical but is the kind which Prior confessed to borrowing from Ferdinand of Cordova, namely, the notion of a 'truth that can no longer be prevented' because the time for preventing it is now past. Consequently, I am not saying it would have been *logically* impossible at b that '"Socrates" refers to Socrates' not have been true at a. I am saying simply that at b it was no longer possible to *prevent* '"Socrates" refers to Socrates' from having being true at a.

For a much more detailed treatment of this argument, see my *From Existence to God,* chapter 3, and 'Future Individuals and Haecceitism', *Review of Metaphysics* 20 (1986): 237–70.

II. Property Instances

The main part of this section will be an argument for *predicate* instances, from which it will be a simple step to conclude to there being *property* instances.

Predicates as Undetachable Expressions

On a Fregean view, the name and predicate in an atomic proposition are related to each other as complete expression to incomplete expression. The terms 'complete' and 'incomplete' derive from Frege, who used them mainly in regard to entities: objects were complete entities whereas functions were incomplete. The notion of incompleteness or unsaturatedness is a difficult one, however, so much so that Frege confessed to being unable to define it, and concluded that he must confine himself 'to hinting at what I have in mind by means of a metaphorical expression; and here I rely on my reader's agreeing to meet me half way.'[1] In regard to the incompleteness of predicates, however, I think we can go beyond merely 'hinting' at how it is to be understood

A predicate is an incomplete expression not simply in virtue of its being part of a proposition, for otherwise each logical part of every proposition

---

1. G. Frege, "What Is a Function" in P. T. Geach and M. Black, *Philosophical Writings of Gottlob Frege* (Oxford: Blackwell, 1960), 115. In "Concept and Object" (p. 55) he makes the same point: '"Complete" and "unsaturated" are of course only figures of speech; but all that I wish or am able to do here is to give hints.'

would be an incomplete expression. Clearly, that is not the case; for a proposition may be part of a complex proposition, and a name may also be part of a proposition, though neither propositions nor names are incomplete expressions. What, then, does it mean to say that a predicate is incomplete? As I shall argue, it means that a predicate is an *unquotable*, an undetachable expression. Unlike a function proper, the incompleteness of a predicate is not to be understood as its being unable to be discerned in its values;[2] rather, although readily discernible in its values (propositions), it is nevertheless not detachable from them. Such is the incompleteness of a predicate that it cannot even be written down except in writing down the proposition in which it occurs.

Geach has long argued for this position. His central point is that, to recognize a predicate that is common to two propositions, it is not enough to recognize merely the *words* they have in common. Rather, one has also to recognize the *pattern* they have in common. Based on this insight, an argument might be constructed thus:

3.24.   No predicate can be recognized in a proposition unless it be recognized as a pattern in that proposition.

3.25.   But, a pattern cannot be detached from that in which it is a pattern.

3.26.   Therefore, no predicate can be detached from the proposition in which it occurs.

In regard to premiss (3.24), the inadequacy of recognizing mere expressions and the correlative need to recognize a pattern is evident in the Polish proposition 'Maria zabiła Jana.' ('Mary kills John'), which contains the same word ('zabiła') as does 'Joanna zabiła Jana.' The 'a' inflection of the verb 'zabił' is determined by the feminine gender of 'Maria' and 'Joanna,' and would be absent if 'Maria' were replaced by 'Janek,' a name of masculine gender. Even on a superficial view the predicate expression and subject expression are so interwoven that they cannot be disengaged from each other. Consequently, it is not even plausible to suggest that their common predicate could be disengaged from the propositions containing it. Even more striking than Geach's examples are some in which subject and predicate are still more closely interwoven, e.g., in the propositions 'Maria uśmiechnęla sie' and 'Jan uśmiechnala sie' ('Maria (Jan) smiled'), in which the difference in gender between the subject expressions 'Maria' and 'Jan' is marked not merely by the presence or ab-

---

2. An example of a function *proper* is the cube function, of which the value for the argument 2 is 8. In that value there is no indication of the function. A predicate is like a function proper in being a mapping, but is unlike it in being clearly distinguishable in its value, viz. in a proposition.

sence of 'a'at the *end* of the verb, but by the presence of 'a' and 'ę' respectively more *internal* to the verb.

The point that predicates are not constituted by words alone can be made more perspicuously still, by showing that they need not be constituted by words at all, but simply by a pattern. For instance, a very limited kind of language might have its names written in lower case, and its predicates indicated by varying the height of one or more letters that compose the names, e.g:

	Possible language	*English translation*
Name:	'christopher'	'Christopher'
Propositions formed	'Christopher'	'Christopher is black'
with the name:	'cHristopher'	'Christopher is wise'
	'chRisTopher'	'Christopher is angry'

In such cases there would be no *words*, nor even any inflection, attached to the name to indicate the presence of a predicate. On the contrary, the predicate would be indicated solely by the pattern of letter heights in the inscription of the name.[3]

We might therefore agree with Geach that, if we think of his (and the other) examples, 'surely the temptation vanishes to regard the predicate . . . as a simple sign with its slots for proper names quite external to it.' The predication is not effected by the bare word 'zabił', nor even by 'zabiła.' Rather, it is effected by the functional expression 'ξ zabił(a) ζ,' which, as he notes, is shorthand for the following:

The name ξ in the nominative case, and the name ζ in the accusative case, are combined with a token word 'zabił', inflected to agree in gender with the name ξ.[4]

At this point it might be objected that, even if there are some languages in which a predicate cannot be recognized without recognizing a corresponding pattern in a proposition, there are others in which that is patently not the case. Surely the predicate common to 'Socrates is wise' and 'Plato is wise' is

---

3. Of course, the names would need to be reasonably long, if we were to obtain even a modest range of predicates. Moreover, if Frank Ramsey were right in thinking that names and predicates are interchangeable, then names might be indicated by patterns of letter heights in the inscription of a predicate. The argument in this book, however, is quite neutral as to whether Ramsey is right or wrong, since it assumes only that the Fregean analysis is at least one legitimate analysis of atomic propositions.

4. P. T. Geach, "Names and Identity" in S. Guttenplan, ed., *Mind and Language* (Oxford: Oxford University Press, 1975), 139.

nothing but the expression 'is wise.' Surely, there is no need to understand the predicate as conforming to some such instruction as the following:

> The name ξ is placed adjacent to, and to the left of, the token phrase 'is wise.'

Indeed not. Admittedly the instruction is both so simple and, to us, so obvious that we may be inclined to discount it as entirely trivial. It may seem that, even without any such instruction, we could perfectly well combine the expressions 'Socrates' and 'is wise' to form the proposition 'Socrates is wise.' That suggestion is not without a grain of truth; for we can make sense even of English that has been severely butchered, and we might well understand a foreigner who reversed the normal word order by uttering 'Is wise Socrates.' However, the intelligibility of butchered English has its limits; and there are many possible patterns that might exceed those limits. A few written examples are given below.

A.   'is wise'

's
e
t
a
r
c
o
S'

B.   'is wise'

                                        'Socrates'

C.   'is wise'   'Socrates'

We may be tempted to regard (A), (B), and (C) as 'unnatural' as compared with the 'naturalness' of our present way of writing English. Yet, no one way of writing it is any more natural than the others. And that should alert us to the fact that, in different circumstances, our present way of writing might have seemed every bit as contrived as (A) seems to us now. Lifelong familiarity with the present pattern exhibited in 'Socrates is wise' should therefore not mislead us into dismissing it as trivial. Hence, the difference between 'Maria zabiła Jana' and 'Socrates is wise' is not that there is some pattern to the former, but none to the latter. Rather, there is a pattern to both: it is simply that the pattern happens to appear to us as more striking in the former, but notably less so in the latter. So, our earlier conclusion remains intact: predicates cannot be detached from the propositions in which they occur. Although in some languages the *expressions* used in forming predicates can be detached, there are no languages in which the *predicates* themselves can be detached or placed within quotation marks.

The position for which I have been arguing can now be set out in more detail:

3.27.   The predication relation — that is, the relation of predicate to name — is essentially that of a pattern added to (or superimposed upon) the name to result in a proposition.

3.28.   Although an atomic proposition is something more than a name, the 'something more' need in principle involve no *words* additional to the name. Even though in practice it will indeed involve more words than a name, those additional words are themselves not the predicate.

3.29.   What, then, is the role of the additional words in (A)-(C) and in the Polish examples? Their role is simply to differentiate what is predicated, e.g., to differentiate between *what* is predicated in 'Socrates is wise' and in 'Socrates is lonely.' As we saw, the same task could be performed solely by variations in patterns (e.g., the heights of the letters in 'Socrates') without any additional words. An obvious disadvantage of that method is that differences of patterns (and, hence, predicates) would be severely limited. Far better, therefore, to retain the one basic pattern for all predications, and to achieve the required differences by means of words, thus providing the possibility of virtually unlimited numbers of predicates. The same predicate *pattern* is to be found in both 'Plato is wise' and 'Plato is lonely.' The difference in *what* is predicated in each case is indicated by the difference in the words used to form that pattern.

3.30.   Although the pattern may be described in words, that description has no place in the proposition, and is not to be mistaken for the predicate.

3.31.   Since what is essential to predication is the pattern that marks a proposition, and since patterns are undetachable from what they are patterns of, no predicate can be *detached* from the proposition in which it occurs. Even in such propositions as 'Socrates is wise' the pattern remains undetachable. By removing the words 'is wise' we do not *detach* the pattern; we simply destroy it.

3.32.   Since the predicate is a pattern that characterizes a proposition, we may also follow Geach by speaking of it as a *feature* of a proposition.

3.33.   The foregoing conclusion suffices to discredit the view that predicates are quotable expressions detachable from the propositions in
which they occur. On such a view, they might have been regarded
as being marked by slots into which names could be plugged to
form a proposition. In that case, 'Socrates is wise' would have been
formed by plugging 'Socrates' into the slot in '____ is wise.' A predicate would thus have been a proposition in waiting, or a proposition manqué so to speak.

It is apparent that the union between the logical parts of a proposition is
quite unlike that between the parts of a jigsaw puzzle or between a socket
and a plug. It is, indeed, a far more binding union, so binding as to be indissoluble. It is indissoluble because one of the parts is not a linguistic entity in
its own right but is entirely parasitic upon the proposition in which it occurs.
Precisely for this reason it deserves to be called an *incomplete* expression. It is
incomplete not in the relatively weak sense in which a wall might be called an
incomplete house or a chapter might be called an incomplete story, an isolated fragment of a story. Rather, it is incomplete in the strongest possible
sense, in that it cannot occur even as an isolated fragment. If it does not occur
in a proposition, it does not occur at all. That means, consequently, that the
predicate can be neither 'is wise' nor '____ is wise'; for obviously each of them
is what the predicate is not, viz. a quotable expression. On the contrary, the
role of 'is wise' is merely to *indicate* or *signal* the presence of a common predicate in 'Socrates is wise' and 'Plato is wise.' The predicate itself, however, is not
quotable: it is not even a proposition manqué such as 'is wise' might have
been thought to be. It is, as Geach says, simply a feature of, or pattern in, a
proposition.

Predicate Sense

It might now be asked whether what has been concluded about predicates is
equally true of predicate sense. For instance, it might be objected that, while the
earlier conclusions apply at the syntactical level, it has yet to be shown that
they are applicable to the semantic level as well. Just because the predicate
expression in 'Socrates is wise' is a feature of the whole expression, why should
a similar relation be claimed between the senses of those two expressions?

The objection ignores the fact that at no stage were we operating solely at
the level of syntax; for at no stage were we concerned solely with expressions
(inscriptions) whether predicate expressions, propositional expressions, or
name expressions. On the contrary, neither 'Socrates is wise' nor 'Socrates' was

taken to be *solely* an expression. The former was taken to be an expression-having-both-a-sense-and-a-truth-value (a proposition), and the latter was taken to be an expression-having-both-a-sense-and-a-semantic-value, and hence as a name rather than a mere inscription. Neither was the predicate mistaken for a pattern in a mere expression but was shown to be a pattern in a proposition, i.e., a pattern in a *sense-bearing* expression. That being so, the argument was conducted at a level that embraced syntax and semantics alike: the relation in question held not between mere expressions but between sense-bearing expressions.

Perhaps, however, the objection might be pressed by urging that, even if our conclusions did concern predicates and propositions (and not just predicate expressions and propositional expressions), that still would not entitle us to conclude that the senses of a predicate were features of the sense of a proposition. To that I would reply with the following argument:

> Our thoughts would be incomprehensible even to ourselves, if their sense structures were impossible to grasp, at least in principle.
> But we have no access to our thoughts independently of the linguistic expressions in which they are expressed; and a fortiori we have no means of grasping the sense structure of the thoughts except by way of the logical (as distinct from grammatical) structure of those linguistic expressions (propositions).
> Consequently the sense structure of those propositions just *is* the logical structure of the thoughts they express; and if it were not, it could never be grasped at all.
> Therefore our thoughts would be incomprehensible even to ourselves, if their sense structure were not the same as the logical structure of the propositions used to express them.[5]
> But our thoughts are not incomprehensible to ourselves.
> Therefore, their sense structure is the same as the logical structure of the propositions used to express them.
> Therefore, since the predicate expression in a proposition is a feature of that proposition, the sense of that predicate will be a feature of the sense of the proposition.

In conclusion, then, the thesis of the predicate's being a feature of a proposition, and undetachable from it, might be illustrated by the non-linguistic

---

5. Naturally, there are as many legitimate sense structures as there are legitimate logical strucures of the propositions used to express them.

analogue of a vase formed from a lump of clay. The resulting vase would conform to a pattern that could have been described in advance. Although that description is of course no part of the vase, the shape to which the description applies not only is part of the vase but an undetachable part as well. The analogy with the predicate is fairly clear, though, like all analogies, it should not be pressed too far. The lump of clay may be likened to the name 'Socrates,' and the vase to the proposition 'Socrates is wise.' The shape of the vase may be likened to the predicate in the proposition, and the expression '___ is wise' (or the description 'A name is placed to the left of, and adjacent to, the token expression "is wise"') may be likened to the description of the pattern that is embodied in the vase. The predicate is no less a feature of the proposition than is the shape of the vase; and it is no more quotable or detachable from the proposition than is the shape detachable from the vase.

The Existence of Predicate Instances

One consequence of the incompleteness or unquotability of predicates is that, even though we may well continue using descriptions like 'the predicate in "Socrates is wise"' in referential position, we should at least be so aware of the logical impropriety of doing so as to eschew its misleading ontological implications. The only referent appropriate to a description in that position is an object, i.e., a complete entity. Hence any use of 'the predicate' in that position would be appropriate only if it referred to a complete entity, albeit a linguistic one, e.g. a *quotable* expression like 'is wise.' In saying, for example, 'The predicate in "Socrates is wise" is the same as the one in "Plato is wise",' we would leave ourselves open to the question, 'And just which one is that?' Yet, any such question is as unanswerable as 'Which philosopher was that?' would be, if asked in response to 'Socrates was a philosopher.'

What, then, are we to say about the use of a description like 'the predicate in "Socrates is wise"'? The first thing to say about it is that it is no less misleading ontologically than the TV advertisement 'Brand X puts whiteness back in your sheets.' It is misleading because, just as the use of 'whiteness' might suggest that whiteness is an (abstract) object, so the foregoing use of 'predicate' might suggest that a predicate, too, was an object, albeit a linguistic object, a quotable expression. The second thing is that, just as the TV advertisement can be reframed to avoid any suggestion of whiteness being an object, so the use of 'predicate' can be reframed to avoid any suggestion of a predicate being a complete (i.e., quotable) expression. In the former case, the result would be 'Brand X makes your sheets white again.' In the latter case it would be,

3.34.   Socrates is what is said of Plato in 'Plato is wise.'[6]

or

3.35.   What is said of Socrates in 'Socrates is wise' is what is said of Plato in 'Plato is wise.'

There are two points to note about (3.34) and (3.35). One is that the expression 'what is said about Socrates in "Socrates is wise"' is always substitutable both salva veritate and salva congruitate for 'is wise.' For precisely that reason it is not to be construed as occurring in referential position; and, consequently, it could offer no ground for the kind of improper questions noted above. The other point is that, even in (3.35), neither the expression 'what is said of Socrates in "Socrates is wise"' nor the expression 'what is said of Plato in "Plato is wise"' occurs in referential position; for the 'is' which links them functions neither as a copula nor as the 'is' of identity. Rather, it indicates the presence of a *second*-level predicate '____ is . . . ,' from which (3.35) is formed by filling the slots with first-level predicables.

As can be seen, the possibly misleading way of speaking is avoided only at the price of verbosity and inelegance. Naturally, we are quite free to choose the more concise and more elegant, but possibly misleading, use if we wish. However, we are no more free to embrace its misleading ontological implications than we are to embrace the misleading implications of using 'whiteness' in 'Brand X puts whiteness back in your sheets.'

The points I have been making are one consequence of accepting the undetachability of predicates. Another consequence is that the predicate-expression-in-'Socrates is wise' and the predicate-expression-in-'Plato is wise' are *not interchangeable*. Why? Because interchangeability would presuppose that the expression occurring in one proposition could be isolated from that proposition and used in a different proposition by being attached to another name. But, predicates are quite undetachable from propositions; and so they could never be interchanged. In any case, they are merely features of propositions; and it clearly makes no more sense to speak of interchanging or transferring features than it does to speak of eating thoughts or drinking wishes.

Two points have now emerged:

3.36.   In one respect, the predicate in 'Socrates is wise' *is* the same as that in 'Plato is wise'; for what is said about Socrates is precisely what is said about Plato.

---

6. Both occurrences of 'is' are of course predicative: neither one is the 'is' of identity.

3.37.   In another respect, the two incomplete expressions are *not* the same; for the one can occur nowhere but in 'Socrates is wise,' whereas the latter can occur nowhere but in 'Plato is wise.'

Although we may be able to make do with the term 'predicate' to capture the first point, we need some other term to capture the second. For that purpose, I introduce the term 'predicate instance.' 'Socrates is wise' and 'Plato is wise' contain predicate instances which are alike both in saying exactly the same of Socrates as of Plato and in doing so by using language tokens of the same type. Nevertheless, the instances undoubtedly do differ, for one can occur nowhere but in 'Socrates is wise' whereas the other can occur nowhere but in 'Plato is wise.' To deny any difference on the grounds that predicate instances could not differ except in regard to sense would be to invoke a semantic version of the Identity of Indiscernibles, and one which is no less misconceived than is the correlative ontological claim that there can be no difference between two individuals except in regard to properties (whether relational or non-relational).

Objections to Predicate Instances

Among objections raised against predicate instances, one maintains that their notion is self-contradictory, and another that the notion conflicts with a point made by Davidson. The first objection goes thus:

> In 'Spot is black' and 'Fido is black,' precisely the same is said of Spot as is said of Fido.
> But, what is said of Spot is the predicate instance in 'Spot is black,' and what is said of Fido is the predicate instance in 'Fido is black.'
> But, the predicate instances are not the same: they are distinct one from the other, as well as being non-interchangeable with each other.
> Therefore what is said of Spot is not the same as what is said of Fido.

Having agreed that what is said of Spot is the same as what is said of Fido, the advocate of predicate instances seems therefore forced to accept that it is not the same.

There would be a contradiction only if what is said of Spot and Fido were to be the same and not the same under one and the same respect. Bearing that in mind, let us recall just how the two predicate instances do differ. Certainly, it is not that Fido is being said to be black, whereas Spot is being said to be only very nearly black: each is said to be unqualifiedly black. The difference between them is that one instance of the predicate can occur only in 'Fido is black,' whereas the other can occur only in 'Spot is black.' The question at issue, therefore, is whether the predicable indicated by '____ can occur only in "Spot (Fido) is black"' says anything about Spot (Fido). It could do so, however, only if it were a first-level predicable. So, the question is whether it really is such a predicable. If it were, our two propositions would be elliptical for:

> 'Spot is black and can occur only in "Spot is black".'
> 'Fido is black and can occur only in "Fido is black".'

If that really were the case, it would be obvious that different things were indeed being said about Spot and Fido. Equally obviously, however, that is not the case. The predicable indicated by '____ can occur only in "Spot (Fido) is black"' is being said neither of Spot, nor Fido, nor of any other individual. Rather, it is being said of a predicable, viz. the predicable indicated by '____ is black.' In other words, it is a meta-linguistic predicate.

Once that is recognized, there is little difficulty in answering the earlier objection. To have been effective, the objection had to show that acceptance of predicate instances entailed that what was said of Spot was both the same and not the same as what was said of Fido. It has now emerged, however, that the claim is untenable. The truth is that precisely the same first-level predicate is said of Spot as is said of Fido. The difference between the instances of that predicate is one not of first-level predicates but of meta-linguistic predicates. What is attributed to Spot is neither more nor less than what is said of Fido. The difference is concerned solely with what is predicable of the *predicate instances* said of Spot and Fido respectively. One of them is said to be able to occur only in 'Spot is black'; the other is said to be able to occur only in 'Fido is black.' Consequently, although the predicate instances are admittedly both the same and not the same, they are the same under one respect and different under quite another. Contrary to the first objection, therefore, acceptance of predicate instances carries no commitment to any contradiction.

The second objection claims the admission of predicate instances to be irreconcilable with Davidson's point that the capacity for the correct use of unsurveyably many propositions is explicable only if those propositions are regarded as derived from a base that is not unsurveyable. The argument for the objection might go as follows:

> The capacity for the correct use of unsurveyably many proposi-
> tions presupposes a base that is not unsurveyable.
> But, the base for atomic propositions is said to consist of names
> and predicate instances.
> But, there are as many predicate instances as there are proposi-
> tions containing them.
> Hence, for there to be unsurveyably many propositions there
> would have to be unsurveyably many predicate instances.
> But, that would contradict the initial premiss that the base pre-
> supposed by the propositions be not unsurveyable.
> Therefore, there can be no such item as a predicate instance.

One defect in the argument is its failure to distinguish between:

3.38.   the base elements employed in the *forming* of an atomic proposition,

and

3.39.   the base elements contained *in* the proposition thus formed.

The base elements employed in forming 'Fido is black' are 'Fido' and some
such instruction as:

> The name β is placed adjacent to, and to the left of, the token
> phrase 'is black.'

The result of following that instruction with respect to the name 'Fido' would
be 'Fido is black,' a proposition which obviously does not contain the instruction, but does contain a predicate the presence of which is indicated by the
phrase 'is black.' Now, it is true that unsurveyably many propositions would
contain unsurveyably many predicate instances. It is not true, however, that
the capacity to *form* unsurveyably many propositions requires a grasp of any
predicate instances at all, let alone unsurveyably many of them. A grasp of
just one such instruction as that mentioned above suffices for forming any
number of propositions.

Nor can it be said that a capacity to use (as distinct from a capacity to
form) unsurveyably many propositions presupposes a grasp of unsurveyably
many predicate instances. That objection could be sustained only if instances
of the same predicate were to say different things about the bearers of the
names to which they were attached. In fact, the contrary is the case; for a capacity to use atomic propositions presupposes merely a grasp of what each
predicate instance says about an individual. As already shown, although predi-

cate instances do differ from each other, they differ not at all in regard to what each says of an individual. Each instance says exactly the same of an individual as does every other instance of that predicate: what is said about Fido by 'Fido is black' is precisely what is said about Spot by 'Spot is black.'

The second objection has been no more successful than the first. The doctrine of predicate instances, which follows straightforwardly from the incompleteness of predicates (their undetachability, unquotability) is neither self-contradictory nor in conflict with the Davidsonian claim. Both objections were vitiated by the tacit assumption that what I have called the semantic version of the Identity of Indiscernibles is true, that the only possible difference between predicate instances is one of sense. There is no more reason to accept that version than there is to accept its ontological version. Quite the contrary.

I should stress that the notion of predicate instance does not purport to be at all explanatory: it does not pretend to make the unity of a proposition any clearer than it already is. It is simply a corollary of recognizing the predicate expression as incomplete in the sense already explained. The notion of a predicate instance would be problematic only if predicate expressions were regarded as complete, i.e., capable of occurring in their own right.

I began this section of the appendix by specifying both its goal and the means by which that would be attained. The goal was to show that there are such entities (albeit incomplete) as property instances. The means I adopted was to follow Frege's view that the ontological categories exemplified in the things we talk about reflect the linguistic categories of the expressions we use to talk about them. The first and major step, therefore, was to determine whether there were *predicate* instances. That having been done, it is a straightforward step to conclude that there are corresponding *property* instances.

Subsistent Existence:
An Identity of Limit Cases

One critic of Subsistence Existence has described it as 'a hinge on which the better part of Aquinas' conception of divine simplicity turns. If we can make sense of that identification, we can make sense of the conception of divine simplicity.'[1] Although the last claim is somewhat overstated, there is no doubt that making sense of Subsistent Existence is indispensable for making sense of divine simplicity. Unfortunately, the ease with which that same notion can be misunderstood or even misrepresented is beyond dispute, as some of the objections to it, including those of the author of the quotation above, serve constantly to remind us. Both misunderstanding and misrepresentation alike can be avoided, however, with the help of the two key notions that have already been introduced. One is that of a limit case, the other is that of an individual's being the bound of its existence.

The Notion of Subsistent Existence

I begin with the previous chapter's conclusion that Socrates' existence is what Socrates bounds, Fido's existence is what Fido bounds, and so on for the existence of each individual. In every case the individual is the *bound*, not the subject, of its existence. Recall that, in respect of *individuation*, Socrates is prior to his existence, which is to say that the individuality of Socrates' *existence* is parasitic on the individuality of Socrates himself. In other words again, in respect of individuation Socrates' existence is incomplete vis-à-vis Socrates.[2] In respect of *actuality*, however, Socrates is posterior to his exis-

---

1. C. Hughes, *On a Complex Theory of a Simple God* (Ithaca: Cornell University Press, 1989), 5. Hughes also confesses to being unable 'to construe Aquinas' claim that God is *ipsum esse* in such a way that it fails to come out necessarily false.'
2. I call *both* Socrates and his existence 'incomplete,' though in different respects. Socrates' existence is incomplete in regard to *individuation*, since it has no individuation in its own right, but solely in virtue of Socrates. Socrates himself is incomplete in regard to *actuality*, since he has no actuality in its own right but solely in virtue of his existence.

tence, which is to say that, in this particular respect, Socrates is parasitic on his existence, and hence that Socrates is incomplete vis-à-vis his existence. Since both relations would be missing if there were no distinction between bound and bounded, our understanding of Subsistent Existence will be better served by considering it not simply as an entity lacking any distinction between bound and bounded, but as an entity lacking each of the two incompletenesses which would have been present, had there been any distinction in it between bound and bounded. For that reason we need to examine the implications of the twofold lack of incompleteness:

4.01. Because it lacks any incompleteness in respect of *individuation*, Subsistent Existence obviously lacks an individuator, i.e., lacks any bound to existence .

4.02. Because it also lacks any incompleteness in respect of *existing*, Subsistent Existence might be regarded as lacking any instance of existence, and hence as a bound that has nothing to bound.

At first sight, there is a striking incoherence about both claims. The first task is therefore to decide whether the incoherence is anything more than merely apparent. So far as (4.01) is concerned, that will depend on how a zero-bound instance of existence differs from instances of existence that are *not* zero-bound. And that in turn will depend on how a zero-bound instance of existence is to be understood. In particular, is it to be understood as simply an infinitely expanded or enriched version of a creature's instance of existence, somewhat as the Universe might be compared with an electron as being an infinitely expanding version of the very limited instance of matter or energy found in the electron?

I mention the case of the Universe because both it and an electron are genuine instances of matter, though differing from each other both in size and complexity. We might, however, be inclined to ask whether a similar point might not be made about a zero-bound instance of existence: are it and Socrates' instance of existence both genuine instances of existence, differing merely in 'size' and complexity? If so, (4.01) would certainly be incoherent in claiming that a zero-bound instance of existence is not incomplete in respect of individuation, since it would be claiming that what was essentially incomplete (namely, an instance of existence) could in fact be complete. To decide the question, however, we need now to recall the notion of a limit case.

Are Limit Cases Relevant to Instances of Existence?

As noted in chapter 1, the limit case of a series is that towards which the members converge when their defining characteristic is progressively varied to the point of extinction. Thus, the limit case of a series of lines is that in which the length of the members has been progressively reduced to zero (a point), and the limit case of a series of regular polygons is that in which the angle through which the sides turn at the vertices has been progressively reduced to zero (a circle). Similarly, the limit case of a series of instances of existence would be that in which a defining characteristic of such instances had been varied to the point of extinction. Before attempting to determine precisely what that might be, however, we need to consider whether instances of existence really can be ordered to form a series, or whether they could never be anything but a collection of unordered members. If the latter, the question of their limit case could not even arise.

Since a defining characteristic of an instance of existence is that it be bounded by an individual, our question is, can the various bounded instances of existence be arranged in decreasing order of boundedness? Of course, that could readily be done if the sum total of *non*-existential property instances had by each individual could be arranged according as they contracted existence less and less.[3] But the difficulty with this proposal is that, even were agreement possible on an ordering of individuals according to degrees of F-ness and likewise in regard to degrees of G-ness, none might be possible in regard to degrees of the conjunctive property F *and* G, since there may be no agreement about the relative weightings to be attached to having F as compared with having G.

If F were intelligence and G were musicianship, how could individuals be rated on a scale according as the conjunctive property F *and* G contracted existence less and less? If that seems impossible, how much more so would it be if we were to take into account not just two properties, but the full range of real properties had by an individual. If there can be no agreement about *that*, surely there can be no agreement about the ordering of the individuals' instances of existence according as their bound is less and less constricting. But if there is no agreement about forming such a linear series, there would seem to be no sense in speaking of those instances as having any limit case.

While all this may be true, it is also irrelevant to the question at issue, which is not whether any particular ordering can meet with unanimous acceptance, but whether any ordering at all (whether unanimous or not) is conceivable. What we have to consider is whether each of us could say that individual b was less limited *qua* individual than c, and so on for all other individuals. If we can do that, albeit with much soul-searching and perhaps

3. For the notion of contracting existence, cf. chapter 3, p. 35.

hesitation about borderline cases, then such an ordering is certainly conceivable. Naturally, our ordering would reflect our own priorities and preferences, but so too would our rating of a list of musical compositions. Yet those preferences do not preclude each of us from ordering the musical compositions from worst to best, though they may well preclude our ordering from being accepted unanimously. The point is that the notion of ordering individuals *qua* individuals is no more questionable than that of ordering musical works, even though it may be incomparably more difficult. What is certainly questionable in either case is merely the notion of a *unanimously* accepted ordering.

I should add that it is not required that we be able to give an account of how we arrive at our ratings, nor that there be no hesitation or doubt about how to rate one or other individual. All that is needed for present purposes is that we know what it would be like for individuals to be so rated. The notion of *b* being more or less limited than *c*, not simply in one respect, but *qua* individual, is therefore not a questionable one; nor is the notion of an ordering of individuals on that basis.

The Limit Case Instance of Existence

Given that the ordering of instances of existence is conceivable, we might wonder therefore whether these instances have any lower limit simpliciter, or whether there is no point in an ordered series of decreasingly bounded instances of existence beyond which there could be yet another instance, one with a still less constricting bound. I raise that conjecture not to pursue it any further, but merely to stress that, even if there were such an instance (a limit simpliciter), it would never be a *totally* unbounded one. Consequently, it would differ only relatively, but never absolutely, from members of the series of which it was the limit simpliciter.

Only a zero-bound instance would differ absolutely from any member of a series of bounded instances of existence. Yet, although differing absolutely from them, it would be precisely that towards which the ordered series points. For just these reasons, a zero-bound instance of existence would indeed be a *limit case* instance of existence. Moreover, even if there were total disagreement about the particular order of precedence among the series' members, the mere fact of their being conceivable in *some* order of precedence guarantees that the limit case will always be the zero-bound instance of existence, no matter how the members might be linearly ordered. So, the notion of a limit case instance of existence is acceptable, irrespective of there being any *unanimity* about the order of precedence in the series that points towards it.

It has now to be noted that there is no univocity whatever, not even par-tial, between 'instance of existence' in 'zero-bound instance of existence' on the one hand and in 'bounded instance of existence' on the other,[4] for the zero-bound instance of existence would no more be an instance of existence than a circle is a polygon, or a zero-place predicable is a predicable. And that is why, notwithstanding appearances to the contrary, there is merely an ap-parent incoherence in (4.01); for, although it would be self-contradictory to say that an instance of existence was complete in respect of individuation, there is no contradiction in making that claim about a *limit case* instance of existence.

The same conclusion can be drawn about (4.02), for what has been said about an instance of existence that was not incomplete in respect of indi-viduation could be said, mutatis mutandis, about a *bound* of existence that was not incomplete in respect of existing. Although it is part of the notion of a bound of existence that it be incomplete in respect of the existence it bounds, it is no more contradictory to speak of a bound that is not incomplete than it is to speak of a predicable that is not incomplete, namely, a zero-place predi-cable. A zero-place predicable is not a contradiction in terms precisely be-cause 'predicable' is here being used in the alienated sense on which I have remarked more than once. Similarly, a bound of existence that is not incom-plete in respect of existence is not a contradiction in terms, precisely because in that context 'bound of existence' is being used in an alienated sense. And just as 'zero-place predicable' referred not to a predicable but to a logical item in which there was no predicable incompleteness whatever (a proposition), so likewise 'bound of existence that is not incomplete in respect of existence' refers not to a bound of existence but to an entity in which there is no incom-pleteness in respect of bounding. That, however, is just another way of speak-ing of a bound of existence that bounds no instance of existence. Hence, (4.02) too is innocent of incoherence.

Only One Limit Case Instance of Existence

Given that it does make sense to speak of there being a limit case instance of existence, we need now to consider whether there might not be more than one such case. This question might be thought to arise if the series were a branching one; it might also be thought to arise if there were parallel series of instances of existence, each with its own limit case. According to the first sug-gestion, instances of existence would belong to the one series up to a certain point, beyond which they would split into two or more distinct branches. Ac-

---

4. As I shall argue in chapter 8, that is not to say that the two uses are totally equivocal or merely casually ambiguous.

cording to the second suggestion, instances of existence might be considered as divided between two or more series that have no members in common. If there were different limit case instances of existence for each series, and if God were supposed to be the limit case of a series of instances of existence, we might then be embarrassed to find ourselves having to recognize a veritable pantheon of deities.

My first response is that I am not concerned with ordering instances of existence according to any *evolutionary* series to which their bounding individuals might belong. Rather, I am concerned only with ordering them conceptually, quite irrespective of any evolutionary series to which they might belong. I therefore deny the need to consider the possibility of multiple series since, once it is accepted that instances of existence *can* be ordered conceptually according to their decreasing boundedness, there is no reason to think that they could not be *conceived of* as all belonging to one and the same series.

However, let us suppose that, per impossibile, they really did have to be conceived of as forming multiple series. Any limit case of these series would have to be a zero-bound instance of existence. I say this because, as already noted, a limit case instance of existence could not be an instance of existence in any univocal sense of that term. In this way it differs absolutely from even the most slightly bounded instance of existence, for the latter would still be an instance of existence in the univocal sense of that term. Therefore, if any of the supposed multiple series were to have a limit case (rather than merely a limit simpliciter), that limit would have to be devoid of any bound, and hence would be a zero-bound instance of existence.

The question then is whether these multiple series would have the *same* limit case, the same zero-bound instance of existence. Let us therefore assume that each series really did have a different zero-bound instance of existence. To say that they are different instances, however, is to say that they are individuated, each of them being an individual instance of *zero-bound instance of existence*. And, to say that they are individuated is to say that they are bounded. So, the assumption that there could be more than one zero-bound instance of existence is disqualified by its entailing that they could not be zero-bound instances of existence after all.

Subsistent Existence as an Identity of Limit Cases

Having cleared each of (4.01) and (4.02) of incoherence by explaining both of them in terms of limit cases, we might now consider the implications of their being jointly true. About Socrates we have been able to say that, in respect of individuation, he was complete vis-à-vis his existence and, in respect of actuality, he was incomplete vis-à-vis his existence. So, both the bound of his existence and the instance of existence that it bounded were incomplete, though under different respects. Now, the *limit case* of incompleteness in respect of individuation (the limit case *instance* of existence) has proved to be an entity in which there is no such incompleteness, one in which existence has no bound. And the limit case of incompleteness in respect of actuality (the limit case *bound* of existence) proved also to be an entity in which there is no such incompleteness, one in which no bound is actualized by an instance of existence. Clearly, an entity in which existence has no bound is identical with an entity in which no bound is actualized by an instance of existence.

It has thus emerged that the negative claim of *lack of distinction* between an instance of existence and its bound in Subsistent Existence entails the positive claim that in Subsistent Existence an instance of existence and its bound are *identical*. There is thus no problem in maintaining that Subsistent Existence is an entity in which its quiddity = its existence, or an entity in which what exists = its existence. The reason is simply that the left-hand side of these claims is to be understood as 'the limit case bound of existence' and the right-hand side by 'the limit case instance of existence.' Hence, the claims translate into the following:

> The *limit case* bound of existence = the *limit case* instance of existence.

This would be self-contradictory only if it implied:

> Some bound of existence = the instance of existence which it bounds.

But, because 'limit case' is an alienans adjective, there is no such implication: a limit case bound is not a bound at all, nor is a limit case instance of existence any instance of existence. Consequently, there is no difficulty in maintaining that the very same entity is both the limit case bound of existence and the limit case instance of existence.

To sum up. The notion of Subsistent Existence depends crucially on the twin notions of a limit case on the one hand, and of a bound of existence on the other. With the help of those notions, the frequently derided notion of Subsistent Existence proves to be derivable from the notion of any individual in the following very straightforward way:[5]

---

5. Of course, it is one thing to derive the notion but quite another to determine whether there exists anything corresponding to the notion. My present concern is purely with elucidating the notion of Subsistent Existence, not with establishing that there really is such a being, for that was the task of my *From Existence to God*.

Start with the recognition of Socrates or Fido as an individual that
is related to its instance of existence as bound to bounded.

Form the notions of the *limit case* instance of existence and of the
limit case bound of existence.

Note that the two notions have the identical referent.

The notion of Subsistent Existence, then, is the notion of the entity
which is jointly and identically the limit case instance of existence and the limit case bound of existence.

Misleading Notions of Subsistent Existence

Once Subsistent Existence has been understood in terms of the identity between these two limit cases, it is not difficult to recognize the potential for
being misled by such descriptions of it either as 'pure existence,' or as 'pure actuality' (actus purus), or as 'the object that is identical with its existence.' The
notion of pure existence might be thought to suggest an instance of existence
that was neither Socrates',' nor Fido's, nor any other individual's either. To accept that suggestion, however, would not be to attain the notion of Subsistent
Existence, an entity that is said to exist necessarily. Rather, it would be to attain the notion of an entity which necessarily could not exist at all, namely, an
instance of existence that was not the existence *of* anything whatever. On the
one hand, it would not be an instance of existence unless it were the existence
of something; on the other hand, it could not be a *pure* instance of existence
unless it were unbounded and thus not the existence of anything. Hence, the
idea of arriving at the notion of Subsistent Existence by conceptually strip-
ping some *non*-subsistent instance of existence of all bounds or 'impurities' is
one that should not even be entertained, let alone pursued.[6]

The preceding point, however, seems to have escaped Keith Ward, who
professes to think that the notion of a God who is identical with his existence
entails that 'the sort of being that exists when God exists is simply existence.'
This leads him to dismiss the notion with the comment that '"existence" is
just not an answer to the question, "What exists?"'[7] This is exactly the kind of
reasoning which has long bedevilled discussion of Subsistent Existence. Although true in regard to *non*-limit case instances of existence, it is quite irrelevant to their limit case. In regard to the latter, the answer to 'What exists?' is
not 'existence,' but rather 'the entity which is jointly and identically the limit
case instance of existence and the limit case bound of existence.'

6. Equally to be shunned is the less tempting conception of creaturely existence as simply a contracted or bounded version of Subsistent Existence.

7. K. Ward, *The Concept of God* (Oxford: Blackwell, 1974), 157.

Having raised the possibility of being misled by the description of Subsistent Existence as 'pure existence,' I freely acknowledge that the danger is not inescapable. Indeed, it is readily avoidable, provided that 'pure' is understood as 'zero-bound' and the existence in question is not thought to be something that is in any way *shared* with the whole range of instances of existence had by everything from an electron to Socrates, but is understood as simply that towards which the series *points*, its limit case.

Subsistent Existence has a long history of being known as Actus Purus (pure actuality), which is perfectly correct, but which is open to being misconceived as a being in which all potentialities are fully actualized. What is amiss with such a construal? Simply that no such being could differ absolutely from other members of the series of which it purports to be the limit case. Indeed, there could no more be an absolute difference between it and them than between a machine that never ceased operating to its full potential and one that *could* operate in that same way but perhaps had never operated even once. Subsistent Existence or Actus Purus cannot be marked by any potentiality whatsoever, not even by potentialities that are always fully actualized. To say that Subsistent Existence is zero-bounded is not to say that all its potentialities are actualized to the full but that it has *no potentialities at all* to be actualized.

Although there is a perfectly proper way in which Subsistent Existence can be presented as 'pure existence' and as 'Actus Purus,' there is no way at all in which it can be presented as 'the object that is identical with its existence.' Indeed, that would be as nonsensical as describing a proposition that has *no* proper logical parts[8] (e.g. 'Fulgură')[9] as an identity between a subject expression and a predicate. Since subjects and predicates are logical expressions that differ in kind, it would have made just no sense to say that they ever could be *identical* with each other. And it would have been equally nonsensical if, after contrasting 'Fulgură' with a proposition like '$(\exists x)(x$ is a dog),' the former had been described as one in which a first-level predicable and a second-level

---

8. A proper logical part of a proposition is any logical part of it that is not identical with it.

9. 'Fulgură' is a Romanian proposition that may be translated into the Latin 'Fulgurat' or the English 'It lightens' or 'It is growing light', as one might say at the approach of dawn. The interesting thing about 'Fulgură', however, is that it contains nothing corresponding to the suffix 't' in Latin nor to the dummy subject 'it' in English, i.e., nothing with a referring role. On the contrary, it is neither more nor less than a verb *stem*, and hence contains nothing that could be construed as referring to anything of which 'lightens' or 'is growing light' might be predicated. For that reason it is an excellent example of a logically simple proposition.

predicate were identical with each other, for that is precisely what they never can be. Mutatis mutandis, the same can be said about Subsistent Existence. To describe it as an *object* that is identical with its existence would be absurd, since an object is precisely the kind of ontological item that differs absolutely from its existence, and hence could never be identical with it. There is no absurdity at all, however, in denying any identity between any *non*-limit cases (e.g. Socrates and his existence), while at the same time affirming an identity between the limit cases themselves, which is precisely what is required by the notion of Subsistent Existence.

The Ontological Richness of Subsistent Existence

In the last chapter I argued that existence was the richest of properties. It is therefore a major step towards appreciating the ontological richness of Subsistent Existence to have shown that it should be understood as the zero-bound instance of *existence*. Thus understood, it can now be used to rebut Kenny's view of the doctrine of Subsistent Existence as one marked by 'sophistry and illusion' in its claim that pure *esse* (Subsistent Existence) is 'a totality which has no parts, and its "richness" is its entire lack of any property.'[10] Expanding on this criticism, he adds that 'if told simply that Flora *is*, I am not told whether she is a girl or a goddess or a cyclone, though she may be any of these. But God's *esse* is *esse* which permits no further specification. Other things are men or dogs or clouds, but God is not anything, he just is.'[11]

Reason for the Ontological Wealth of Subsistent Existence

Before considering Kenny's conclusion I should draw attention to two ways in which his attempt to simplify Aquinas' doctrine has in fact served to distort it. The first is the claim that Subsistence Existence entirely lacks any properties. Although it is true that Subsistent Existence *has* no properties, it does the reader no service to omit Aquinas' claim that Subsistent Existence *is* (identical with) its instances of *all* the so-called pure perfections, i.e., properties which *in se* bespeak no potentiality. The omission cannot be dismissed as inconsequential since, provided it makes sense, it completely undercuts Kenny's charge that the doctrine is 'sophistry and illusion.' In the following chapter I shall argue that it makes perfectly good sense, and that Subsistent Existence is identical with Subsistent Wisdom and all other limit case instances of the pure perfections.

10. A. Kenny, *Aquinas* (Oxford: Oxford University Press), 1980, 59–60.
11. Ibid., 58.

Kenny's second distortion lies in his suggestion that 'other things are men or dogs or clouds, but God is not anything, he just is.' The partial truth in this claim is that God cannot be assigned to a genus, whether human, angelic, or any other. Kenny fails to add, however, that much can indeed be said *of* God, e.g., that he is wise, omniscient, omnipotent, omnibenevolent, and so on. It can also be said that he is no more distinct from these attributes than he is from his existence. So, it is seriously misleading to depict the doctrine of Subsistent Existence as restricting us to the severely cryptic proposition 'God is [or exists].'

In his defence, Kenny could perhaps argue that his omissions do nothing to invalidate his conclusion about the vacuousness of the notion of Subsistent Existence for, if God is not distinct from his existence and if existence is the most impoverished of properties, nothing is added to him by saying that his omnibenevolence, his omniscience, his omnipotence are also *identical* with so impoverished a property instance. Obviously, the damage would have been done by the initial lack of distinction between God and his existence, which none of the subsequent qualifications could possibly repair. Why? Because even without relying on his own idiosyncratic view of '____ exists,' and even had he conceded both that it was a first-level predicable and that existence was a *real* property, Kenny could still have argued that a God who was identical with his existence must be the least significant of entities. In fact, so long as an object's existence was conceived of as *inhering* in the object, any ontological richness possessed by an existing object could have been attributed only to the object rather than to its existence. An instance of existence that was Subsistent Existence, and hence not inhering in any object at all, would therefore be utterly lacking in ontological riches and hence condemned to languish irretrievably at the bottom of the ontological scale.

Notwithstanding any initial plausiblity, however, such a defence is vitiated by its tacit assumption that an object's existence is inhering in it rather than being bounded by it. Once that assumption is jettisoned and an object's existence is recognized as *bounded* by the object, its existence has to be accepted as more or less rich, depending on the extent to which it is contracted by the individual that both bounds it and individuates it: the less restrictive the bound, the richer the instance of existence that is individuated by it. Consequently, if the bound were relaxed or loosened to the point of extinction, the corresponding instance of existence (Subsistent Existence) would be quite literally rich 'beyond all bounds.' To have turned on its head Kenny's misconception of *existence* is therefore also to have turned on its head his damaging misconception of *Subsistent Existence*. Rather than being the ultimate in on-tological poverty, it is the ultimate in ontological wealth.

In What the Wealth of Subsistent Existence Consists

If we were considering a human as compared with an electron, the richness of the former might have been described in terms of the multiplicity and/or quality of its property instances vis-à-vis those of an electron. No answer in these terms is possible in regard to Subsistent Existence since it is a *zero-bound* instance of existence; and that is to say not merely that it is not an instance of existence but also that no instances of any other properties could belong to it unless they too were zero-bounding. Consequently, the richness of Subsistent Existence is not to be understood in terms of which property instances could belong to it, for clearly none could. Rather, it is to be understood in terms of which *zero-bounding* property instances could belong to it. To be a little more concrete, let F_n, F_{n+1}, F_{n+2} . . . be property instances such that F_n is less con-stricting than F_{n+1}, which in turn is less constricting than F_{n+2} and so on. Let F_o be the instance that places no restrictions at all on whatever has it, and hence would be the limit case instance of F, the zero-bounding instance of F. The question then would be not whether F_n, F_{n+1} F_{n+2}, and so on could belong to Subsistent Existence, but whether F_o could do so.

Although it has yet to be established whether any *non*-existential proper-ties at all do have limit cases that are zero-bounding, nevertheless we can say even now what the limit cases of some property instances would be like — should there prove to be any. More specifically, we might infer that, if there were a limit case instance of power, it might arguably be zero-bounding. The argument would have first to establish that power was what Aquinas called a 'pure perfection,' namely, a property that was not *inherently* limiting. If so, there could be a series of instances of power, each member of which was less and less constricting on the individual that had it. The limit case would there-fore be one which was not constricting at all, one that was zero-bounding. But, if it were zero-bounding, it could not be part of a bound, for that would be to say that part of a bound did *not* bound. So, the limit case instance of power could be zero-bounding only if it were not part of any bound, i.e., only if it were not instantiable in any individual. The question of whether there really are any properties whose limit case instances are *not* bounding is irrele-vant to the present discussion, which has been purely hypothetical. It will, however, be a major topic in the next chapter.

Assuming, then, that there really is a zero-bounding instance of power, how would it be related to Subsistent Existence? To answer that, let us recall the kind of relation that holds in *non*-limit cases, e.g. between Socrates' instance of power (P_s) and his instance of existence (E_s). Two points should be noted:

4.07. P_s is a property instance which is incomplete with respect to Socrates as its individuator.

4.08.   In virtue of being individuated by Socrates, P_s contributes to the bounding of E_s. Besides being completed by Socrates, therefore, P_s is completed also by E_s, albeit in a different respect. In regard to Socrates the completion is in respect of individuation, in regard to E_s the completion is in respect of actuality or existence.

So much for the non-limit cases. The point to be noted about the limit case P_o, however, is that it would differ from P_s precisely in being a zero-bounding instance of power, which means that it would *not* be incomplete with respect to its existence. But, as remarked earlier in the chapter, what is not incomplete with respect to its existence is simply Subsistent Existence. Subsistent Existence would therefore be identical with P_o or, as we may now call it, Subsistent Power. And, in general, any property F that admits of a zero-bounding limit case would be identical with Subsistent Existence, and thus could also be said to be Subsistent F.[12]

The answer to our earlier question, 'In what does the ontological richness of Subsistent Existence consist?', is therefore that Subsistent Existence is the entity in which all *zero-bounding* limit case property instances are united in being identical with each other and with the limit case instance of existence. For reasons mentioned earlier, the identity between these limit case instances is perfectly consistent with *lack* of identity between *non*-limit case instances of those same properties.

Objections

Some criticisms of the notion of Subsistent Existence rely on the assumption that existence is not a real property of individuals. About them no more need be said here, for they were rebutted in the previous chapter where existence was shown to be not only a real property but also the richest of real properties. Three other objections, however, do require attention here.

---

12. The very same conclusion might have been surmised on other grounds, namely, the a priori expectation that the relation between limit case property instances would itself be a limit case relation; and identity might well be described as a *limit case* relation, which would mean that it would not be a relation at all in any univocal sense.

Whether Subsistent Existence Is Unintelligible

Prior has dismissed the notion of Subsistent Existence as being simply unintelligible. Commenting on 'God is his existence' being formed by filling the gaps in '____ is . . .' with a concrete term ('God') on one side and an abstract term ('his existence') on the other, he condemns it as being 'just bad grammar, a combining of words that fails to make them *mean*—like "Cat no six".'[13] Were we to accept his line of argument, however, we should be hard put to account for the success of so many advertisements in print, radio, and TV. If such claims as 'Brand *X* puts whiteness back in your sheets' were meaningless because their authors were logically so unlettered as to combine abstract with concrete expressions, advertising companies should long since have gone bankrupt. That their businesses are booming is due to the fact that even those who may well be affronted by grammatical and logical howlers in advertisements are also perfectly well aware of what they mean. 'Brand *X* puts the whiteness back in your sheets' translates very simply into 'Brand *X* makes your sheets white again.'

Before dismissing 'God is his existence' as unintelligible we might try doing with it what we can do so readily with TV advertisements: we might try translating it into a form which does not offend either our grammatical or our logical susceptibilities. There are two ways of doing so, one of which relies on the notion of limit cases, and one which does not. The first and much the simpler way is merely to recall that 'God is his existence' translates into 'God is the entity in which the limit case bound of existence = the limit case instance of existence,' a proposition which is *not* open to Prior's reproach since the gaps on either side of '=' are not filled by expressions of different kinds.

A second way of translating 'God is his existence' would be to express it not as an affirmation of identity but as a denial of distinctness, namely, 'God is not distinct from his existence.' Now, even if there is some dispute as to whether the latter proposition is true or not, it is not difficult to show that it is intelligible. We have only to recall that a predicable '*F*' cannot be meaningful unless 'not-*F*,' too, is meaningful. 'Red' cannot be meaningful unless 'nonred' is, nor 'intelligent' unless 'stupid' ('non-intelligent') is, nor 'adroit' unless 'clumsy' ('non-adroit') is. Similarly, '____ *is* distinct from his existence' cannot be meaningful unless 'is *not* distinct from his existence' is also. Now, the former occurs in 'Socrates is distinct from his existence,' a proposition which is far from unintelligible, since it implies simply that 'Socrates does not exist' is not self-contradictory. Obviously, then, the predicable '____ is *not* distinct

---

13. A. N. Prior, "Can Religion be Discussed?" in A. Flew and A. Macintyre, eds., *New Essays in Philosophical Theology* (London: S.C.M. Press, 1955), 5.

from his existence' must be meaningful also. Now, 'God is identical with his existence' is merely another way of saying precisely what is said by 'God is not distinct from his existence,' And, because the latter employs a meaningful predicate, the former does too.

The preceding argument might be summarized as follows, in which 'F-ness' does duty for 'existence':

> 'God is his F-ness' is intelligible if 'God is not distinct from his
>   F-ness' is intelligible.
> 'God is not distinct from his F-ness' is intelligible if the predicable
>   '____ is not distinct from his F-ness' is intelligible.
> The predicable '____ is not distinct from his F-ness' is intelligible if
>   the predicable '____ is distinct from his F-ness' is intelligible.
> The predicable '____ is distinct from his F-ness' is intelligible
>   if the proposition 'Socrates is distinct from his F-ness' is
>   intelligible.
> But, the latter is intelligible, since it implies merely that 'Socrates is
>   not F' is not self-contradictory.
> Therefore, all the foregoing conditions have been met for 'God is
>   his F-ness' to be intelligible.
> Therefore, 'God is his existence' is intelligible.

If either one of the foregoing arguments is correct, it would be entirely inappropriate at this point to insist that the notion of anything being identical with its existence is *inconceivable*. Of course, if 'inconceivable' were merely being used loosely to mean 'unimaginable,' the claim would be incontestable, for there are many situations that are unimaginable without being also inconceivable. Thus, a non-existing Socrates is unimaginable, even though perfectly conceivable, since that is just what we do conceive of when we say 'Socrates does not exist.' Again, although we cannot imagine black swans being simultaneously non-black, we have no difficulty in conceiving of it, as we do in saying 'Black swans are non-black.' Although false, self-contradictory propositions are not meaningless. The same kind of point can be made in regard to something being identical with its existence. We need to distinguish between imagining it and conceiving it; and, though the former is impossible, the latter is not. Indeed, that is exactly what we do when we attach to 'God' the predicable '____ is not distinct from his existence.' Conceivability is independent of imaginability, no less than it is of truth. And God's being identical with his existence is quite conceivable, irrespective of whether it be true or false, imaginable or unimaginable.

Whether Subsistent Existence Would Be a Property Instance

Those who misconstrue the simplicity of God as identifying him with existence simpliciter have objected that it would present him as being a property, and hence as an abstract entity rather than a concrete one. As many have noted, however, no such conclusion would follow God's being identical with *his* (instance of) existence; for property instances are not abstract but concrete. But this move too has problems since, 'if every property instance is merely a feature of something more fundamental than itself, then God would be a feature of something ontologically more fundamental than himself. This would be little better than the view that God is an abstract object.'[14]

One response has been to suggest that God is an instance of a 'rich property,' which has been explained as 'a conjunctive property which includes all and only the essential and accidental properties of some individual thing. . . . What then is [an individual like] Giles? An instantiation of the appropriate rich property. Giles is a property instance.'[15] Like Giles, God too would be an instance of a rich property, albeit one which 'has but one element — *being a Godhead* —, which is the same property as *being omniscient, being omnipotent,* and all the rest.'[16] On this account, the property instance of *being existing* would presumably be included in 'all the rest'.

Mann does indeed have a point, but it is one which could readily have been made without invoking rich properties. It could have been made by employing Geach's distinction between *substantival* terms (or count nouns) on the one hand and *adjectival* terms on the other,[17] the former being terms which may occupy both subject position and predicate position, whereas the latter are restricted to predicate position alone. 'Brown' is an adjectival term, since it can occur solely in predicate position, as in 'Socrates is brown.' 'Dog' is a substantival term, since it may be used in both 'Mary was bitten by a dog' where it is a common name[18] and in 'Fido is a dog' where it is not a name but

14. T. V. Morris, *Anselmian Explorations* (Notre Dame: University of Notre Dame Press, 1987), 103.

15. W. Mann, "Divine Simplicity," *Religious Studies* 18 (1982): 467.

16. Ibid.

17. Although 'substantival' and 'adjectival' are part of the grammarian's vocabulary, they are being used here not to make a merely grammatical point but a logical one. See P. T. Geach, *Reference and Generality* (Ithaca: Cornell University Press, 3d. ed., 1980), 63.

18. To say that 'dog' occupies subject position in 'Mary was bitten by a dog' is not to deny that 'Mary' does so also, for there are two subject/predicate analyses of 'Mary was bitten by a dog', depending on whether we ask 'Who was bitten?' or 'What bit Mary?' 'Mary' is a subject term vis-à-vis '____ was bitten by a dog' as predicate, whereas 'a dog' is a subject term vis-à-vis 'Mary was bitten by ____' as predicate.

a predicate. In regard to the former it would make good sense to ask, 'Which dog bit Mary?', unlike in the latter case where it would make no sense at all to ask, 'Which dog is Fido?' Although the predicative use of 'dog' in 'Fido is a dog' might seem to indicate that the property of being a dog is individuated by Fido, the subject use might seem to indicate that it is not. So what is the truth of the matter?

The answer is relatively simple. Yes, being a dog is indeed a property, but only if 'property' is understood in the very broad sense in which I have been using it, as *whatever* is attributed to something by a predicate. However, use of that umbrella term should not obscure the various distinctions that fall under it, e.g., between first-level and higher-level properties, formal and non-formal, Cambridge and real, etc. The fact that 'dog' can occupy either referential or predicative position whereas 'brown' cannot should alert us to yet another distinction, and make us wary of treating Fido's being a dog and his being brown as instances of the *same kind* of property.

Admittedly, Fido's being a dog and his being brown are alike in some respects, namely, in being first-level, non-formal, and real. They do, nevertheless, differ markedly in their relation to Fido for, if Gamma is Fido's instance of being brown, then the property of being brown is instantiated *by* Gamma, but instantiated *in* (i.e., particularized by) Fido.[19] The property of being a dog, however, is instantiated *by* Fido, but is not instantiated *in* anything at all. That is to say, Fido does not particularize this dog but is identical with it: Fido simply *is* this dog. It is the one individual that *is* this dog, but *has* Gamma and many other property instances besides. That is why it would be highly ambiguous, albeit not incorrect, to call this dog a *property* instance. To avoid that ambiguity, however, we might call it a 'primary substance.'[20] Whatever force Morris' objection may have had was gained precisely by ignoring that ambiguity, and cannot survive the recognition of a distinction between substantival and adjectival properties. Perhaps Mann's notion of a rich property can be regarded as a tacit admission of that distinction, for a rich property could do the job he wants of it only if it included one substantival property. In the case

19. Here I am employing a distinction that is recognized by many Aristotelians and Trope theorists alike, despite their each ascribing a different ontological status to property instances. The distinction is between two relations had by property instances, one being the relation between an instance and the *universal* which it exemplifies, and the other the relation between an instance and the *individual* in which the exemplification occurs. For example, the universal property of wisdom could be exemplified *by* an instance w_1, and this exemplifying instance would occur *in* the individual to which it belonged.

20. In adopting this Aristotelian term I am neither affirming nor denying that Aristotle uses it in the same way.

of Giles the substantival property would have been that of *being a man* (or an animal); in the case of God it would have been that of *being a Godhead*.

Although Mann's strategy succeeds against Morris, it does not succeed absolutely, for it allows God to fall under some count noun, e.g., 'Godhead.' Thus, God is allowed to be an instance of some species or genus, a consequence that is inconsistent with the absolute transcendence of the God who is Subsistent Existence. The difficulty is not that Godhead would have to be instantiable exactly once, for the notion of a property being instantiable exactly once is entirely unexceptionable. Rather, the difficulty is that there is no reason why Godhead should not have been instantiated by some God other than the one that did instantiate it. The property of being the first person on the Moon was in fact instantiated by Neil Armstrong but could equally have been instantiated by Mary Smith or any other individual, provided only that she were the first person on the Moon. Similarly, even if it were conceded that Godhead had *necessarily* to be instantiated and that it could be instantiated only exactly once, there is no reason why it should have been instantiated by *our* God. Any (though admittedly only one) being that instantiated it would have been God, though not necessarily the God we now have. So, God would not be a necessary being after all; for, even if there had necessarily to be *some* God, there would have been no need for him to be the God we do have. Moreover, his transcendence would be severely diminished: he would not transcend *all* possible beings, since those possible Gods would presumably be no less exalted than he is. This is the price that Mann has paid to rebut Morris; and it is too high.

The price paid by Mann is one from which the limit case view of divine simplicity is exempt. In reply to Morris' suggestion, it has to be said that God's being 'a feature of something ontologically more fundamental than himself' does not at all follow from 'every property instance is merely a feature of something more fundamental than itself.' His conclusion would follow only if God's existence were a property instance, which Morris obviously thinks the simplicity doctrine is bound to say it is. As we have seen, that is precisely what the doctrine is committed to denying for, in maintaining that God's existence is a *limit case* property instance, it is saying that God's existence is no more a property instance than negative growth is growth. So, Morris' objection lapses.

If Subsistent Existence, Then No Creatures?

It might be objected that the very notion of a zero-bound instance of existence seems to preclude any coexistence between God and creatures, and would place us in the unenviable situation of having to opt either for a God with no creatures or for creatures with no God. As for the first option, it might be suggested that precisely because it lacks any bound, a zero-bound instance of existence would be impotent to exclude any instances of existence but would have to include them all. Since nothing could lie outside it, there could be no beings other than Subsistent Existence; and a God that was Subsistent Existence could therefore have no creatures. This suggestion is reminiscent of the following argument proposed as a 'disproof of the existence of God':[21]

> God is a being than which nothing greater can be conceived.
> Therefore God is unlimited.
> If God is unlimited there can be no other beings.
> There is at least one other being.
> Therefore God does not exist.

Exactly this kind of conclusion, then, might seem to follow if God were the zero-bound instance of existence.

As for the second option, the argument is that, since a zero-bound instance of existence could exclude no actuality whatever, it would have to include material actuality. But, whatever is material either does have a spatial bound or, if infinite, *could* have been bounded at some point. So, a zero-bound instance of existence would apparently have to *include* actualities that were or could be bounded, in which case the putative zero-bound instance of existence could not be necessarily zero-bounded. At the very least, therefore, all material actuality would have to be excluded from a zero-bound instance of existence. But surely there could be no such exclusion unless the putative zero-bound instance of existence did have a bound after all. Paradoxically, therefore, to say that God was Subsistent Existence would be to say that there was no God, only entities that were less than divine.

Each of the opposing options rests on what might seem to be the eminently reasonable assumption that a zero-bound instance of existence is an instance of existence that, precisely because it has no bounds, should exclude no actualities. However, a zero-bound instance of existence is a *zero-place* property instance; and a zero-place property instance is no more a property instance than a zero-place predicable is a predicable. Consequently, a zero-place instance of existence can no more be said to include instances of one-place (or higher-place) properties than negative growth can be said to embrace growth. The two arguments based on the contrary view are therefore entirely specious.

21. I. Weeks, "A Disproof of the Existence of God," *Sophia*, 29, no.3 (1990): 21–28.

The foregoing remarks would fail to impress those like Christopher Hughes who deny that there are any such items as instances of properties, or individu-alized properties.[22] Such people would be able to argue that, since there are no property instances, then a fortiori there could be no limit cases of prop-erty instances. Consequently, there could be no Subsistent Existence con-ceived of as the limit case instance of existence. Even if Hughes were correct about property instances, it would be irrelevant so far as the notion of Sub-sistent Existence is concerned, for the notion of a limit case would be equally viable even if the notion of property instances were not. Rather than talk of property instances, we could talk about the different *degrees* in which the one property could be realized or exemplified in different individuals. Thus, Socrates may have been less wise than Plato but more courageous, and so on for their respective exemplifications of a whole gamut of properties.

Although it is of course possible that some properties were exemplified in each to precisely the same degree, that too is irrelevant to the point I am illus-trating, which is merely that the same properties *could* be exemplified in many different degrees. Instead of talking of Socrates' instance of *F*, Plato's instance of *F*, and Aristotle's instance of *F*, we could talk of the degree to which *F* was exemplified in Socrates, Plato, and Aristotle respectively;[23] and that alone would suffice to validate the notion of a *limit case* exemplification of properties for which there could be no limit simpliciter. Since the notion of a limit case exemplification of existence is all I require for the notion of Sub-sistent Existence, the objection to it that stems from an aversion to property instances is misconceived. I am not, however, impressed by opposition to property instances, but have explained and defended them in the Appendix to chapter 3.

Conclusion

The conclusion to be drawn from the foregoing thrust and counter-thrust be-tween the antagonists is not that the notion of Subsistent Existence should be abandoned, but that the disputants have been labouring mightily in attacking and defending a straw man. They have been struggling to make sense of God's being identical with existence or, alternatively, of God's being identical with

22. Hughes, *On a Complex Theory of a Simple God*, 10–20.
23. I am far from implying that different property instances really are only different degrees of a property. All I am suggesting is that some of the same conclusions can be reached irrespective of whether we employ property instances or degrees of a property.

his existence, whereas the simplicity doctrine is in no way committed to the former. Nor, even, is it committed to the latter, unless 'his existence' be understood as 'the limit case instance of existence,' a point that seems to have escaped the critics.

Once 'his existence' is understood as 'the limit case instance of existence,' the notion of Subsistent Existence is impervious to any of the aforementioned criticisms. As the limit case of the richest of properties, it can scarcely be reproached with being the most vacuous or impoverished of beings. Nor can it be rejected as an abstract entity, for although first-level properties as such may be abstract entities their *instances* can undergo change, and hence are concrete. Finally, as the limit case instance of existence, it is a zero-bound instance of existence, and thus cannot be criticized as being 'a feature of something ontologically more fundamental' than itself. Perfectly good sense can therefore be made of the notion of Subsistent Existence.

As remarked at the beginning of this chapter, making sense of Subsistent Existence is a necessary condition for making sense of the divine simplicity. It is not, however, a sufficient condition, for there is also the task of making sense of the identity between Subsistent Existence and the various properties that are commonly attributed to God. This will be addressed in chapter 5 and in chapter 6 together with its associated appendix.

5

Subsistent Existence and
Its Non-Existential Properties

As mentioned in the first chapter, the notion of Subsistent Existence is one from which all the other tenets of the divine simplicity can be inferred, and most notably the identity between God and each of his non-existential properties. In this chapter, therefore, I shall be making good some of that claim by arguing that the God who is identical with the limit case instance of existence is identical also with the limit case instance of a number of *non*-existential properties.

I begin by recalling that both 'zero-bound' and 'limit case' are alienans adjectives[1] which means that, even though Subsistent Existence is a *zero-bound* instance of existence, a *limit case* instance of existence, there is no instance of existence which it is—just as there is no instance of growth which negative growth is. For just that reason Subsistent Existence is an entity to which the categories of individual and property instance are strictly speaking not applicable. Nevertheless, it is precisely from a knowledge of entities to which those categories are indeed applicable that we can gain further insight into the notion of Subsistent Existence. I say this because, as I indicated in the previous chapter, if LC is the limit case of a series of entities *a, b, c, d, . . .*, then

> 5.01. the kind of entity that LC is will be correlative to the kind of entities that are members of the series,
>
> *even though*
>
> 5.02. LC differs absolutely, and not merely relatively (whether in degree or even in specific difference), from the members of the series.

From the conjunction of (5.01) and (5.02) it follows that the knowledge of LC that can be gleaned from its role as a limit case will be comparatively slight. In such limit cases as a circle or a zero-place predicable, however, this

---

1. For the notion of an alienans adjective, see chapter 1, n.4.

would be of no concern since our knowledge of them is quite independent of our knowing them to be limit cases of anything. Not so in regard to Subsistent Existence, for we lack the direct knowledge of it that we do have of a circle. We are thus in no position to scorn whatever knowledge can be derived from its being the limit case of one or more series of property instances. Although slight, such knowledge is not only indispensable, it is also invaluable since it is knowledge of the one who created us.

I spoke of 'one or more series' of property instances because it is no part of the notion of a limit case that it be restricted to being the limit of merely one series. This is evidenced by a circle's being the limit case not only of a series of regular polygons but also of a series of circular-shaped figures formed from dots which are ever closer to each other as the series approaches its limit case. Hence, the mere fact that Subsistent Existence is the limit case of a series of instances of existence is itself no bar to its being the limit case of one or more series of instances of other properties. Our immediate task, therefore, is to establish whether that is in fact the case. If so, it will be not simply Subsistent Existence, but Subsistent F, Subsistent G, Subsistent H, etc., where F, G, H are non-existential properties.

Concerning *non*-limit case instances of existence, we know that their ontological richness is manifested by the kind of bound they possess, i.e., by the individuals that bound them. The less constricting the bound is, the richer will be the existence that it bounds, a richness that may well be expressed primarily by the quality of those properties rather than by the sheer number of them that the bound allows. Thus, even if an electron were to have a greater number of properties than Einstein, that would not make its existence richer than his. Moreover, it is not impossible that there be beings superior to any member of the human species, and consequently that the bounds on their instances of existence would be rather less constricting than any possible human bound, thus exhibiting properties distinctly more exalted than human ones. So, perhaps some instances of existence could be extraordinarily richer than any to be found among humans, and hence more closely approaching the zero-bound instance of existence. In general, the richer an instance of existence is, the more closely it approaches its limit case.

As for the limit case itself, it has to be said that its richness could not be manifested by even the most exalted of property instances, for property instances are individuated by individuals, and individuals *bound* their existence. Hence, to say that the richness of the limit case instance of existence could be manifested by property instances would be to say that it was bounded, and therefore not a limit case at all. Yet, if no property instances can manifest its richness, in what does its richness consist? In considering that question, recall that the limit case is not to be conceived of as an instance of existence which has per impossibile been stripped of its bound, for a bounded instance of existence could not survive without a bound, and an unbounded instance of existence conceived of in that way would be a contradiction in terms.[2] On the contrary, the zero-bound instance of existence is not simply an entity that lacks a bound, but one for which a bound is simply not possible. To say that it is a zero-bound instance of existence is to say that the notions of bound and bounded, or of an individual and its existence, are simply inapplicable to it.

What is it, then, that does for the limit case instance of existence what the non-existential property instances do for any *non*-limit case instance of existence, namely, manifest its richness? A clue to the answer has already been provided in the preceding chapter, where Subsistent Existence was shown to be an entity in which the limit case *bound* of an instance of existence was identical with the limit case *instance* of existence. What has now to be done is to spell out what a limit case bound of an instance of existence is. Since a (*non*-limit case) bound of an instance of existence is simply an individual, a limit case bound of an instance of existence is a limit case individual. However, *pace* bare particular theories, there can be no individuals without property instances. Consequently, a limit case individual will have *limit case* instances of whatever property instances are compatible with its being a limit case individual, i.e., with its being zero-bounding. But there could be no zero-bounding individual unless its properties too were zero-bounding, and therefore were identical not only with it but with each other. So, the richness of Subsistent Existence would be manifested in its being identical with as many limit case instances of properties as would impute no bound to it. We may now expand our earlier account of Subsistent Existence as follows:

> Subsistent Existence is the entity in which the limit case *instance* of existence = the limit case *bound* of existence = the limit case instance of F = the limit case instance of G = the limit case instance of H = . . .

2. If it should seem paradoxical to say this while at the same time claiming that Subsistent Existence is unbounded, I merely note that the paradox turns on the ambiguity of the phrase 'instance of existence.' As used in '0-bound instance of existence' or in 'limit case instance of existence' its meaning has been alienated from the way it is used in 'Socrates-bounded instance of existence.' Consequently, there is no more contradiction in speaking of such an instance of existence being unbounded than in speaking of a (rocking) horse being inanimate. As used in 'instance of existence that has been stripped of its bound,' however, its meaning has *not* been alienated; and so that phrase is inescapably self-contradictory.

What has yet to be determined is just what can be substituted for '*F*,' '*G*,' and '*H*.' It will not suffice that the substitutes merely have limit case instances for, in order to be identical with Subsistent Existence, those limit cases must also be *zero-bounding*.

Which Attributes Are Divine?

Among theists of the Western tradition God is commonly thought to be all-powerful, all-wise, all-knowing, all-good, all-merciful, all-just, to mention just a few of his attributes. He is also thought to be immaterial; and that precludes his having any attributes that would presuppose his being material. Consequently, he could have neither size, shape, limbs, temperature, dexterity, and so on. Although Western theists are in reasonable agreement as to which properties God has and which he does not, they disagree as to the criterion to be used in deciding that issue. They disagree also as to whether the difference between divine and human attributes is an absolute one or simply one of degree or perhaps of specific difference. I shall touch upon these questions as a brief prelude to setting out a case for a small sample of the attributes that the limit case account of the divine simplicity allows us to ascribe to God.

The Perfect-Being Account vs. the Limit Case Account

As remarked in the first chapter, perfect-being theologians attempt to derive the divine attributes from their notion of God as an absolutely perfect being, a being 'than which nothing greater can be conceived.' From this it is said to follow that God will have whatever attributes it is better to have than not to have or, as their adopted mentor Anselm put it, 'whatever it is better to be than not to be.'[3] In comparatively recent times such attributes have come to be called 'great-making properties,' and the conclusion drawn is that God exemplifies a maximally consistent set of such properties. The rule for determining whether God has any property *P* would therefore be simply this:

> If having *P* contributes to the excellence of a thing that does have *P*, then an absolutely perfect being has *P*; otherwise the being does not have *P*.[4]

According to Anselmians, it is not enough to say that God has the maximally consistent set of the great-making properties, it has also to be said that

---

3. Anselm, *Proslogion*, parts V–VI.
4. G. Schlesinger, *New Perspectives on Old-Time Religion* (Oxford: Oxford University Press, 1988), 16.

he has all such properties to the maximum degree. This presupposes that there is in fact a degree of intelligence, an intrinsic maximum, which nothing whatever could exceed.[5] It should be remembered that the intrinsic maxima are not conceived of as limit case instances of properties, but are merely what I have called limits simpliciter.

For good or ill, one conclusion to be drawn from the Anselmians' thesis is that God's attributes are at least generically the same as ours. This cannot be gainsaid by insisting that God has P to the maximum degree, while Socrates has P only to a lesser degree. On the contrary, if God is P to the maximum degree, then a fortiori he is P. Hence, although God and Socrates would not both exemplify P to the *maximum* degree, they would both exemplify P. This seems to be one consequence of ascribing to God the so-called great-making properties. That consequence is by no means inevitable, however, for it could readily be avoided if 'perfect' in 'perfect P' or 'infinite' in 'infinite P' or 'omni' in 'omnipotence,' 'omniscience,' or 'omnibenevolence' were taken to function as alienans adjectives, i.e., if a perfect, or infinite, or omni instance of P were taken to be a *limit case* instance of P. Since there is no evidence, however, of perfect-being theologians having ever held that the intrinsic maxima were anything but limits *simpliciter*, we are entitled to conclude that the attributes they ascribe to God are at least generically the same as some human ones, and hence that the divine attributes would be simply human attributes writ large.

Even though Aquinas does use terms like 'perfect P,' 'infinite P,' and 'omni-P' in discussing the divine attributes, his conception of them as 'pure perfections' effectively precludes his regarding them merely as human ones writ large. P is a pure perfection, however, if and only if it is not necessary that it be characterized by any potentiality, i.e., imperfection. On the other hand, P would be a mixed perfection if it were necessarily characterized by at least some potentiality. For example, Aquinas takes intellection to be a pure perfection, meaning thereby that, although it is sometimes characterized by potentiality (in the case of human intellection), potentiality is not a necessary feature of it: it is not a feature of intellection *as such*. Sensation he regards as necessarily

---

5. Perfect-being theologians are apt to ascribe to Anselm the view that God's properties are intrinsic maxima of the great-making properties. William Mann has even tried to ascribe it to Aquinas but, in doing so, failed to accord due weight to Aquinas's insistence that the pure perfections occur in God in a *supereminent* mode. W. Mann, "Divine Simplicity," *Religious Studies*, 18 (1982): 458–60.

Neither is Richard Swinburne immune from conceiving of divine properties as merely maxima of human ones. Speaking of God as 'pure, *limitless*, intentional power,' he notes that such power is 'the maximum *degree* of a kind of causality (known intimately to ourselves when we perform intentional actions).' *The Christian God* (Oxford: Oxford University Press, 1994), 152. Emphasis mine.

characterized by potentiality, and thus as a mixed perfection. He allows only pure perfections to be ascribed to a God who is Actus Purus or Subsistent Existence, and in whom they have to be understood as lacking in any potentiality.

The limit case account of divine attributes, however, offers us an alternative and perhaps simpler route to Aquinas' conclusion. Indeed, that conclusion is simply a corollary of what it means to say that the divine *F*-ness is the limit case of instances of human *F*-ness; for the distinguishing mark of a limit case just *is* that it differs absolutely from the members of the series of which it is the limit case. *Pace* the Anselmians, therefore, *no* attribute of God can be even generically the same as its creaturely counterpart, for it is only the *limit case* instances of creaturely attributes that can be ascribed to him.

The immediate task now is to determine which, if any, human attributes admit of limit cases that are zero-bounding, and thus have to be ascribed to an entity on whose existence there neither are, nor could be, any bounds. Do instances of power, knowing, intellection, willing, wisdom, goodness, love, mercy, justice and so on have limit cases that are zero-bounding, and therefore should be ascribed to God?

A Common Strategy for Determining the Divine Attributes

Before examining any attribute in particular, it is worth sketching the basic strategy that is to be followed in each case, viz.

5.03.   For any creaturely attribute *F*, the first question is whether it has a limit case. Because the limit case terminates an *ordered series* of instances of *F*, the question cannot be answered without first specifying in what respect the instances can be *ordered*.

5.04.   The next step is to determine just where such a series is heading, i.e., what, if anything, might be said to be its limit.

5.05.   If the series does in fact have a limit, the next question is whether it is a limit case or a limit simpliciter.

5.06.   However, even if there does prove to be a limit case instance of *F*, we cannot assume that it will be zero-bounding. The final step, therefore, is to determine whether it is zero-bounding, and thus ascribable to Subsistent Existence.

Expanding on (5.06), it has to be said that Subsistent Existence could be unbounded only if it were susceptible to no external influences at all, whether in regard to what it is or in regard to what it does. The point is, of course, that susceptiblity to any external influences would itself constitute a potentiality, and hence a bound on an entity that ex hypothesi could have no bounds. Subsistent Existence is therefore precluded from being a material entity, since all such entities are susceptible to external influence: they can be acted upon in various ways. Even an immaterial entity, however, would be open to external influences if what it understood, knew, or did were in *response* to its experience of something external to it. The question raised by (5.06), therefore, is this: Which limit case instances of properties commonly ascribed to God can be had by him without imputing to him any susceptibility to such external influences?

The general strategy I have outlined can be used to determine which of a wide range of attributes may be ascribed to God. To consider each and every one of them, however, would distract from the main thrust of this book. For the purposes of illustrating how the strategy works in practice, it will be enough to test it on three attributes, namely, power, knowing, and intellection.

Omnipotence

What is the series of which omnipotence might be some kind of limit? Presumably it would be a series of instances of powers in which increasingly more of the effects produced was due to the power employed and increasingly less to the materials on which the power was expended. Suppose that the effect being sought were the constructing of a jumbo jet aircraft. A manufacturer might proceed in various ways, depending on how much of the aircraft he allowed to be prefabricated by others. Obviously, less power would be employed by the builder if *all* the parts were prefabricated, and the builder's job were merely one of assembly. The more that the builder himself had to produce, the greater the effort he would have to expend. Vastly more effort would be required if he were to manufacture all of the parts, more if he were also to convert raw materials into the metal sheeting, cables, plastic, and other materials being used in the parts, and more again if he were also to extract the raw materials from the ground. With a little imagination this series might be extended further, with the constructor having to consume ever more energy as his initial materials became ever more basic. It is not difficult to see where the series is heading: it is heading towards the case where the constructor has nothing whatever to work on, the case in which *all* the causality comes from him and none at all from his using any preexisting materials. In this case the constructor would have to produce the aircraft from *nothing*: far from being a mere constructor, he would be a creator.

Since creation is the limit towards which the series is pointing, we want now to know whether it is a limit simpliciter or a limit case instance of power. Is it essentially the same kind of power as that exemplified by the members of the series, or is it not? Now, it has to be remembered that in every member of the series a necessary condition for the exercise of power is that there be something for the power to be exercised *on*. It matters not how insignificant that 'something' might be; the simple fact is that, without it, even the most awesome of powers would ipso facto be rendered nugatory. Far from being nugatory, however, the limit towards which the series of those powers is pointing is a power that is utterly impervious to the absence of anything on which to operate, for it is precisely the kind of power that is geared solely to the production of effects that are *not* produced by acting on any preexisting entity. The kind of power exemplified in members of the series could therefore be conceived of as approaching this limit as closely as we might please, but with as little chance of ever attaining it as any regular polygon has of being a circle. As in the circle example, the limit of the series of powers is not a limit simpliciter but a limit case.

For our purposes what has to be noted is that, precisely because the limit case instance of power requires no materials whatever on which to operate, nothing could ever frustrate or inhibit its exercise, nor even modify the effects of its exercise. In producing its effects it is wholly independent of anything else; and that means that the limit case instance of power can be ascribed to Subsistent Existence without thereby imputing any bound to it.

Some might be tempted to object that, if this were the kind of power belonging to Subsistent Existence, he would be precluded from intervening in an already existing Universe. Why? Because surely that would be a case in which the 'raw materials' (the Universe) would already be there to be operated on. What the suggestion overlooks is that, even if the Universe or parts of it might be regarded as raw materials relative to the actions of its inhabitants, never at any moment in its history does it have the role of raw materials relative to Subsistent Existence.[6] Subsistent Existence is its creator not just at one moment, but at every moment of its existence; it is *continuously* being sustained in that existence by his creative power, in the absence of which the Universe would vanish without trace.

Obviously, what might have been thought of as an intervention in the Universe would not be an operation on something that, once having been created, existed in its own right at every moment thereafter. Rather, it would

6. Strictly speaking, it is no more logically proper to say 'God causes the Universe to continue to exist' than it is to say 'God causes the Universe to begin to exist,' for both locutions suggest that God acts *on* the Universe, when there could be no Universe to act upon. Properly, they should be written respectively as 'God causes it to be that (the Universe continue to exist)' and 'God causes it to be that (the Universe exist).'

be simply the continuing creation of the Universe that was now in some modified state relative to its immediately preceding one. None of this effect would stem from any 'raw materials': the *whole* effect—the Universe in its new state—would stem from Subsistent Existence. This, of course, is not to endorse occasionalism, for occasionalism takes the role of a creature, *X*, in the production of any effect to be either totally non-causal or merely instrumental. A creator God, however, simply cannot act in that way, the simple reason being that he has neither *X* nor anything else on which to act. What he can do is to bring it about that (*X* be or do *F*). In such circumstances the causality of *X* would not be instrumental but secondary. I merely mention this point here, but shall develop it at some length in chapter 7.

Having said earlier that the limit case instance of power can be ascribed to Subsistent Existence, I should now add that it is entitled to be called 'omnipotence', though not primarily because it is so much 'greater' than any creaturely power. Nor is it called 'omnipotence' simply because of the boundless *number* or *diversity* of the effects it can produce, although this is the aspect that tends to monopolize contemporary discussions of the topic.[7] Rather, it is entitled to be called 'omni-potence (*all* power)' because it is responsible for *all* of any effect it produces: no part of its effects is due to there being any materials in which it is produced. If the effect were an aircraft, then *all* of the machine down to the last electron or subatomic particle would have been produced by such a power: no raw materials, let alone any more sophisticated equipment, would have contributed anything at all. This is omnipotence not only in the most literal sense of the word but also in its most profound sense.

Knowing

Before asking whether there is any limit case instance of knowing, let us first consider an artificial language, and let us suppose its inventor to have decreed its vocabulary to be invariable. We now construct a series of knowings in the first of which a language learner knows just one word from the vocabulary, in the second two words, and so on until the final member of the series is a knowing which embraces the complete vocabulary. Because of our supposition, the last member is a knowing not simply of all the words that are in fact

7. Examples are T. Flint and A. Freddoso, "Maximal Power," in their *The Existence and Nature of God* (Notre Dame: University of Notre Dame Press, 1983), 81–114; P. T. Geach, *Providence and Evil* (Cambridge: Cambridge University Press, 1977), chapters 1 and 3; A. Kenny, *The God of the Philosophers* (Oxford: Oxford University Press, 1977), chapter 7; G. Mavrodes, "Defining Omnipotence," *Philosophical Studies* 32 (1977): 91–202; E. Wierenga, "Omnipotence," *Philosophy and Phenomenological Research* 43 (1982): 265–76.

in the language but of all that *can* be in it. In this respect it would differ from a similar series constructed for a natural language and in which its last member would be a knowing of all the words which were in fact in that language, but not of all that ever could be in it. For just that reason this last member would not be a limit member, whereas the last member of the series for the artificial language would indeed be a limit. What kind of a limit? Because it differs only in degree from that found in any of the preceding members of the series, it would be a limit simpliciter.

Of course, learners of the artificial language are not the only ones who may know its whole vocabulary, for presumably its inventor does too. There is, however, a significant difference between the two: the learner's knowing is a passive one, but the inventor's an active or creative one. Since learner and inventor both know the same vocabulary, the inventor's knowing of it is no less a limit to the series of knowings than is the learner's. It could not, however, be a limit simpliciter, since its active or creative manner of knowing differs radically from the learner's passive manner of knowing and hence differs absolutely from every member of the series that it limits. In respect of that series the inventor's knowing would therefore be a limit case.

Turning from the restricted vocabulary of an artificial language, let us now consider the true propositions in a natural language, and conceive of a series of knowings in which the first member is a knowing of the proposition p, the second a knowing of the propositions p and q, and so on, culminating in the final member, which is a knowing of what, purely for the purposes of this example, we might suppose to be *all* the true propositions about the Universe. The fact that there were two ways of knowing all the words in the artifical language suggests that it is at least conceivable that there be two ways of knowing all the true propositions in our natural language, namely, passively by discovering them to be true, and actively in bringing it about that they be true.[8] The former would be a limit simpliciter, the latter a limit case.

Could such a limit case be ascribed to Subsistent Existence? Clearly, yes; for, since it contains no element of passivity or dependence, it is perfectly compatible with Subsistent Existence. And, indeed, to say that such knowledge did not belong to Subsistent Existence would be to say that his existence was bounded in some way, and thus that the putative zero-bound instance of existence was *not* a zero-bound instance of existence after all. In the practical

8. This should not be taken to imply that God knows of each proposition that it is true or that it is false. If some propositions are such that they can be neither true nor false, then not even God could know them to be true or know them to be false. He could of course know them for what they are, namely, as neither true nor false.

knowledge associated with his creating and creatively sustaining the Universe, not only would Subsistent Existence's knowledge be creative, it would be all-embracing. In other words, it would be omniscience.

I should emphasize that, although Subsistent Existence is omniscient, his knowledge can be neither complex nor propositional. It cannot be complex, since there can be no complexity in a simple God. Hence, although human knowledge consists of innumerable truths, his consists of a truth in which there are no proper parts. Nor can that truth be propositional. It will of course be the limit case of a propositional knowledge as it increases both in size and degree of integration; but, just as the limit case instance of *F* is not an instance of *F*, so the limit case instance of a proposition will not be a proposition. One reason is the inadequacy of propositions to express even all human knowledge, which is why non-linguistic art forms are indispensable.[9] The more important reason is that a simple God is identical with his knowledge; so that, if his knowledge were propositional, God himself would likewise be propositional.

It turns out therefore that, although it is highly convenient to explain God's omniscience by saying that $(p)(p$ is true $\supset$ God knows that $p)$, it is also highly misleading. It is misleading because it bears the unfortunate connotation of a God who expresses his knowledge in propositions. It is preferable to avoid any such connotation by explaining his omniscience in terms that leave the *mode* of his knowledge entirely unspecified. For just that reason I prefer to say no more than that he is omniscient because he knows all that there is to be known about himself and all else. Although it is clear *that* his knowledge can be neither complex nor propositional, the *mode* of such knowledge is far from clear to *us*. Even if humbling, however, our ignorance should hardly be unexpected if we are serious in affirming an absolute difference between God and creatures.

Intellection

Instances of knowing may manifest varying levels of *understanding* or *intellection*, depending upon how broad or constricting is the theory with which a knower is operating. Let us consider a series in which each instance of intellection is within the context of an increasingly broad theory. Our immediate concern then is to determine just where the series is heading. It is not difficult to see that it is heading towards an intellection which is within the context of

9. This point is illustrated by a remark of Pavlova's. When asked after a performance what she had been trying to convey, she replied 'If I could have said it, I would not have danced it'.

a theory so comprehensive that not only *will* no new kinds of phenomena escape its embrace, but none ever *could* escape its embrace by remaining unintelligible within it.

The next question is whether this limit would belong to a series in which each member is within the context of a theory that is at least partly dependent upon or determined by the kinds of phenomena that it is supposed to accommodate. No matter how advanced such a theory might be, its development would have been governed to some extent by the need to ensure that none of the known phenomena was inimical to its embrace. Moreover, the very fact that a theory had developed in response to some phenomena would preclude there being any *guarantee* that it would be adequate for each and every new kind of phenomenon. Consequently, since every member of the series under discussion is within the context of a theory that was developed at least partly in response to known phenomena, none of the intellections in it could ever be within the context of a theory so comprehensive as to preclude the possibility of its being unable to accommodate some new kind of phenomenon. That is to say, none of the *member*-intellections could ever be the limit towards which it is heading. That limit would therefore not be a limit simpliciter, but would be a limit case.

What, then, would allow us to say of some theory that no possible new kinds of phenomena ever *could* fail to be accommodated by it? Presumably, the theory would have to be one which was in *no way* a response to phenomena, a theory formed without regard to the experience of any phenomena at all. Yet, if it were in no way a response to phenomena, how could it be guaranteed to accommodate whatever kinds of phenomena might occur? Only if its capacity to accommodate such phenomena were itself a presupposition of their occurring. That is to say, only if the phenomena were a response to the theory rather than the theory being in some way a response to phenomena. This limit case instance of intellection would therefore be one that was independent of phenomena. As such, it would impute no bounds to its possessor, and hence could quite properly be ascribed to Subsistent Existence.

There remains the difficulty that, even if the theory could be conceived of before phenomena occur, it could not be known to be *true* until they did occur. Thus the kind of intellection that had seemed ascribable to Subsistent Existence might, on reflection, seem not to be ascribable to him, since it would entail the kind of *knowledge* that would require him to 'check' with phenomena to discover whether his theory was true. This disquieting suggestion ignores the possibility of phenomena being conceived of neither prior to their occurrence, nor in response to their occurrence, but precisely *in* their being caused to occur. Knowledge of this kind is called 'practical knowledge,' and is the kind that is open to a God who causes everything that exists or occurs. Thus, the fact that even he cannot conceive of an individual *before* it exists does not mean that he can conceive of it only *after* it exists. Rather, he conceives of it precisely in causing it to exist. Consequently, the limit case instance of knowledge can safely be ascribed to God without imputing to him any dependence on anything external to him, nor therefore any distinction in him between bound and bounded.

Conclusion

Of the two main questions considered in this chapter, one concerned which properties could be ascribed to a God who is Subsistent Existence. The other concerned the grounds for saying that *instances* of those properties were identical with Subsistent Existence and with each other, despite the properties *as such* being quite distinct from each other. The answers to these questions were implicit in the two key conclusions from earlier chapters, namely, that existence is not received by an individual but is bounded by it, and that the limit case instance of property F is not an instance of F. The first conclusion entailed that existence was the richest of properties. And that grounded the further inference that a zero-bound instance of existence would embrace all and only those properties that would impute no bound to it, namely, whatever properties could have limit case instances that were zero-bound*ing*.

A zero-bounding property instance could fail to place any bound on Subsistent Existence only by being *identical* with it. Yet, how could there be identity between *limit case instances* of properties if there were no identity between the properties *as such*? The objection is a familiar one, and would be insuperable if God's properties were simply the maxima of great-making properties. On that view, divine simplicity as understood in terms of identity between God's properties would have to be abandoned, and perhaps understood as merely the unity obtaining among God's properties.[10] Since there can be

---

10. Immink feels forced to take this step. 'In the classical doctrine of God the "identity thesis" serves to emphasize the *unity* between God and his perfecting properties. God is *essentially* good, just, and the like. However, we must not defend this unity in such a strong sense that it results in a strict identity between all God's perfecting properties. All we need to say on this point is that God has his divine properties *essentially*.' F. G. Immink, *Divine Simplicity* (Kampen: Uitgeversmaatschappij J. H. Kok, 1987), 175–76. Emphasis in the original.

property unity without property identity, it might have been argued that this move had the merit of retaining a desirable consequence of the latter while freeing us from the allegedly undesirable consequence of God's being so transcendent as to be 'indescribable' and 'totally beyond our grasp.'[11]

On the limit case account, however, the divine simplicity entails neither the identity of properties as such nor the *total* incomprehensibility of God. To recognize God's properties as being limit cases rather than maxima is to see that the putatively insuperable objection is not insuperable after all; for, although lack of identity between properties as such would preclude any identity between their property instances, it would not preclude identity between their *limit case* property instances. It is thus possible to hold not only to the unity of God's properties but to their identity as well. Indeed, the limit case account has the additional virtue of showing God to be absolutely transcendent rather than merely relatively so, which was all that the maxima or limit simpliciter account could allow. As for fears that he would be so transcendent as to be indescribable and totally beyond our comprehension, these can readily be allayed since it is precisely the limit case account of God's properties that offers us the simplest of arguments for the analogical character of God-talk, as I shall show in chapter 8.

The upshot, then, is that the God who is identical with the limit case instance of existence can equally be said to be identical with the limit case instance of power, of knowing, and of intellection, and indeed of any other properties that are not *inherently* limiting, i.e., marked by potentiality. In other words, this God is not only identical with the zero-bound instance of existence, he is identical also with the zero-bound*ing* instance of each of those non-existential properties. Or, in other words again, he is identical not only with Subsistent Existence but also with Subsistent Power, Subsistent Knowing, Subsistent Intellection, and so on.

11. For example, by Immink, in ibid.: 'Aquinas did conclude that they are all identical in God, but this conclusion is not required by the theological notion of God's unity. It is a consequence of Aquinas' overaccentuation of God's otherness. . . . the "identity thesis" is a remnant of the logical models which were used, and is also a consequence of a mistaken idea of God's transcendence.'

Richard Swinburne, too, thinks that the identity thesis is 'quite unnecessary', since the unity of divine properties can be guaranteed by other means (*The Christian God*, 162). This quite misrepresents the rationale of the identity thesis, which has nothing to do with unity in the wider sense, and everything to do with the special unity which is identity. The point is that only a being that is identical with its existence (and hence with its other real properties) can be the *creator* of the Universe.

Thus far, I have refrained from replying to the numerous objections to the doctrine of the divine simplicity. I do so in some detail, however, both in chapter 6 and in its Appendix. The responses do more than merely defend the doctrine; they add considerably to our understanding both of it and its implications for the nature of God.

6

Further Insights
into the Divine Nature

The primary concern of the last chapter was with the divine properties considered as the limit case instances of such creaturely properties as have been described as 'pure perfections.'[1] Descending somewhat from that level of generality, the present chapter elaborates on some aspects of two of those properties, God's cognition and his willing. The opportunity for doing so is provided by five of the objections that have been spawned by those incredulous at what the simplicity doctrine proposes about the divine nature.

I. Divine Cognition

What Omniscience Does Not Imply

It might be tempting to think that, if God is omniscient in all possible worlds, then whatever he knows must be true in all possible worlds. It is a temptation to which Tom Morris seems to have succumbed in an objection to the simplicity doctrine based on a putative incompatibility between the necessity of God's being omniscient and the contingency of some of the things an omniscient being would be expected to know.[2] Rebutting his objection will provide some insight not only into God's mode of knowing but into the implications of omniscience. Morris' argument might be expressed as follows:

6.01.   If property *F* is exemplified contingently, God will have the property of knowing that it is so exemplified.

6.02.   But, if God is simple, the property of knowing that *F* is exemplified is identical with his omniscience.

6.03.   But God's omniscience is essential to him.

1. Recall that pure perfections are properties the notion of which does not entail any notion of potentiality.
2. T. Morris, *Anselmian Exploration* (Notre Dame: University of Notre Dame Press, 1987), 114.

6.04. Therefore, the property of knowing that *F* is exemplified is essential to God.

6.05. But God is a necessary being.

6.06. Therefore, it is a necessary truth not only that *F* is exemplified, but that it is exemplified by the particular object which otherwise appeared to have it only contingently.

6.07. Therefore, not only is the actual world the only possible world, but all our properties are essential.

Before I respond to this argument, some precision must be introduced into the notion of God's omniscience, first by recalling from chapter 5 that it is not to be thought of as an *ability* to know whatever is to be known. To say that God *can* know whatever is to be known would be a misleadingly loose manner of speaking, since it would impute to God an ability or potentiality which in fact it is impossible for a simple God to have. His omniscience is not even a fully exercised ability or a fully actualized potentiality. Rather, it is his actually knowing whatever is to be known without, however, his having any ability to be exercised or any potentiality to be actualized.

The second clarification bears upon how a simple God knows what he does know. Primarily he knows himself and, precisely in knowing himself, he knows everything he himself *does*. He therefore knows himself as creating Socrates, as bringing about the exemplification of *F*, and so on. It has to be added, however, that he does not know Socrates only after having created him, as an artisan might view his work after having completed it, for in that case God's knowledge would be passive vis-à-vis Socrates, and that would be inconsistent with his being the zero-bound instance of existence. Rather, he knows Socrates in the very act of creating him, by his practical knowledge. The same can be said of his knowledge of all other individuals who have existed or will exist, as well as of everything that happens in the Universe.

The point to be noted from all this is that God's knowing each of his numerous creatures and the various properties they exemplify does not require him to perform multiple acts of knowing. On the contrary, each of these creatures and the properties they exemplify are known by God in precisely the one act of knowing himself qua creating. To deny him this knowledge would be to say that he had only limited knowledge of himself, and hence that the zero-bound instance of existence was, mirabile dictu, a bounded instance of existence. But, as just noted, the multiplicity of *what* he knows is quite consistent with the unicity of his *act of knowing*.

Now, however, it might be objected that, even if multiplicity of *objects* of knowledge does not entail multiplicity of knowings, surely the multiplicity of *modalities* must entail precisely that. Surely the necessity of God's knowing himself and the contingency of his knowing what occurs in the Universe cannot *both* be accommodated within the one act of knowing. Before attempting to pronounce on that claim, we need to be quite clear what it means both to say that God knows himself necessarily and that he knows whatever occurs in the Universe contingently. Consider therefore the following possibilities:

> Possibly (God knows only himself)
> Possibly (God knows both himself and whatever features in U_a)
> Possibly (God knows both himself and whatever features in U_1)
> Possibly (God knows both himself and whatever features in U_2)
>
> .
>
> .
>
> Possibly (God knows both himself and whatever features in U_n)

The necessity of God's knowing himself requires only that he be an object of the divine knowledge in *all* of the foregoing possibilities. Similarly, the contingency of his knowing whatever occurs in U_a requires only that the latter be an object of the divine knowledge in *less than all* those possibilities. Obviously, both requirements are satisfied by the second possibility which, be it noted, does not at all require any multiplicity of knowings. Rather, it requires merely that there be two objects of the one knowing, with one of the objects featuring in all the possibilities and the other in only one of them.

Against the foregoing background discussion of God's omniscience, the flaws in Morris' argument become more obvious. Consider his inference from (6.04) and (6.05) to (6.06). Here he is claiming that, because God's property of knowing that *F* is exemplified is an essential one, and because God is a necessarily existing being, it is a necessary truth that *F* is exemplified. Note, however, that it could be a necessary truth only if an omniscient God were to know it in *all* possible worlds. Note, too, that Morris seems to think that God's knowing it in all possible worlds is undoubtedly entailed by his omniscience being essential to him. Let us see whether this is in fact correct.

To say that omniscience is an essential divine property is to say merely, 'It is essential to God that $(p)(p$ is true $\supset$ God knows $p)$.' From this it does not follow that 'In *all* possible worlds [it is essential to God that (he know p)].' On the contrary, all that follows is the much weaker claim that 'In any possible world *in which p is true* [it is essential to God that (he know p)].' Nor is this claim strengthened by adding that God is a 'necessarily existing being,' for the fact that God exists in all possible worlds does not entail that p is true in all possible worlds. All that follows from (6.04) and (6.05), therefore, is

6.06′. In all possible worlds God exists & in any possible world in which
F is exemplified, it is true that God knows that F is exemplified.

Clearly, (6.06′) offers no grounds at all for saying that it is true in *all* possible worlds that F 'is exemplified by the particular object which otherwise appeared to have it only contingently.' In other words, it is one thing for God to be omniscient in all possible worlds, but quite another thing for everything he knows to be true in all possible worlds. Between these two claims there is no incompatibility, as is evident from the earlier listing of what God would know, had he created universes other than the actual one.

This reply disposes of Morris' objection, but in doing so it suggests two further difficulties. One is that the cognitive state of a God who is free would seem to be merely contingent; the other is that, if God's act of creation is free, it would seem to follow that his knowledge was increased by his creating the Universe.

The Divine Cognitive State Is Contingent

At first sight it might seem surprising to find that the cognitive state of a simple God could be contingent; and that is how it did indeed appear to Brian Leftow, who found it 'hard to imagine how God could avoid having real contingent attributes if he is *essentially* omniscient and the world is as it is *contingently*. For if God is omniscient, God knows all that is actually true. Moreover, if the world were different in certain respects than it actually is, an omniscient God would know this. So if the world is contingently as it is, it seems that God's intrinsic state of knowledge is contingently as *it* is.'[3] Hughes makes much the same kind of point.[4]

Leftow stresses that the claim is *not* 'that if the facts known vary between possible worlds, God is only contingently omniscient. It is rather that God is omniscient *because* he knows everything, so that if God is essentially omni-

3. B. Leftow, "Is God an Abstract Object?" *Nous* 24 (1990): 595. I should add that Mann ('Simplicity and Immutability in God,' *International Philosophical Quarterly* 23 [1983]: 273–74) formulates a similar kind of objection which he then tries to rebut by distinguishing God's cognitive activity from the content of his cognition, and conceding that the latter (but not the former) does vary from world to world. In my view this concession is misconceived.

4. 'Why might one suppose that God must have some intrinsic properties inessentially? An argument to that effect would go like this: since God is essentially omniscient, at every possible world, He knows whatever is true at that world. Because different things are true at different worlds, what God knows must vary from world to world. Knowledge, whatever else it involves, involves belief: so God's beliefs vary from world to world. But if God's beliefs vary from world, so too must his intrinsic properties.' C. Hughes, *On a Complex Theory of a Simple God*, (Ithaca: Cornell University Press, 1989), 108.

scient, the intrinsic cognitive state in virtue of which he is omniscient varies between possible worlds. If in world W God knows that p, God is omniscient in W because he knows (*inter alia*) p in W, and if in W^* God is omniscient because he knows (*inter alia*) $\sim p$, God's intrinsic cognitive state of affairs differs from W to W^*, and so God is in his W-state or his W^*-state only contingently.[5] This is thought to count against God's being simple.

As we shall see, this argument is defective on two counts. The first is its failure to distinguish between two senses of 'contingent,' and to specify which of these is being used in claiming God's cognitive state to be contingent. The second defect is its failure to recognize that, surprising as some may find it, contingency as such is far from alien to a simple God. Let me repeat that *the only contingency that is alien to him is one that would impute potentiality to him.* Consequently, the interesting question is not whether God's cognitive state is contingent, but whether its contingency would impute any potentiality to him.

To repair the first defect, we need first to distinguish the internal contingency in the first of the following propositions from the external contingency in the second:

6.08.   'God contingently has cognitive state$_W$ rather than cognitive state$_{W^*}$.'

6.09.   'It is contingent that (God have cognitive state$_W$ rather than cognitive state$_{W^*}$).'

To test whether either kind of contingency is alien to God, we need then to ask whether either would impute any potentiality to him. Clearly, (6.08) would do so, since it conceives of God as having a potentiality which is in fact actualized by cognitive state$_W$, but which could have been actualized by cognitive state$_{W^*}$. On the contrary, (6.09) has the merit not only of providing a genuine sense of 'contingent' but also of imputing no potentiality at all to God, as explained in (6.10) and (6.11):

6.10.   *Proposition (6.09) employs a genuine sense of 'contingent'* — since it entails 'It is not necessary that (God have cognitive state$_W$), nor is it necessary that (God have cognitive state$_{W^*}$).'

6.13.   *Proposition (6.09), however, imputes no potentiality to God* — since it implies not 'God could have cognitive state$_{W^*}$,' but merely 'It

<hr>

5. B. Leftow, "Is God an Abstract Object?" Where Leftow uses 'P' I have substituted 'p,' and 'W' for 'W'. Leftow uses this argument to question what he takes to be part of Aquinas' simplicity doctrine, viz., 'God does not have attributes which are distinct from one another as contingent and necessary intrinsic attributes are' (594).

could be that (God have cognitive state$_{W*}$).'[6] Since the latter does not entail the former, there can be no objection to this kind of contingency being associated with God.

Bearing these preliminary remarks in mind, we are now in a position to reply to Leftow's objection that God could not be simple because the necessity of his omniscience conflicts with the contingency of his being in a cognitive state$_W$. It should be obvious that the necessity and contingency in question are jointly satisfied by the truth of any one of the possibilities of which the following are but a few.

> Possibly (God is omniscient and is in cognitive state$_W$)
> Possibly (God is omniscient and is in cognitive state$_{W*}$)
> Possibly (God is omniscient and is in cognitive state$_{W**}$)
> Possibly (God is omniscient and is in cognitive state$_{W***}$)

The necessity of God's omniscience requires only that he be omniscient in all possible worlds; and the contingency of his being in cognitive state$_W$ requires only that he be in that state in one of those worlds. Obviously, the necessity of his omniscience conflicts not with the contingency of his *being* in any particular cognitive state, but merely with the possibility of his *changing* from one state to another. Thus, the necessity of his omniscience does not preclude all contingency, but only such contingency as would impute potentiality to God. But that is scarcely surprising, nor is it at all damaging to a simplicity which has been shown to be consistent with a contingency that is expressed by the external use of the modal operator.

The alleged difficulty of denying that God has 'real contingent attributes if he is essentially omniscient and the world is as it is contingently' has turned out to be either superfluous or ineffectual. It is superfluous if directed against a God of whom it would be logically proper to say, 'He could have had cognitive state$_{W*}$.' Since the internal use of 'could' already precludes the God in question from being simple, any objection to simplicity that is based on that use would tacitly assume what it set out to prove. If directed against a genuinely simple God, however, the objection is ineffectual, since it would have to be formulated in terms of 'It is possible that (God have cognitive state$_{W*}$),' the truth of which does not count against God's being simple, since it imputes no potentiality to him. Even a God who is simple can have a cognitive state that is contingent.

---

6. This latter proposition is true *absolutely* speaking, but not true *ex suppositione*. That is to say, on the supposition that God does have cognitive state$_W$, there is *no* possibility of his having cognitive state$_{W*}$.

No Lacuna in God's Knowledge

This conclusion emerges from considering an objection by al-Ghazali and endorsed by R. Burns, who claims that 'if God's "essence" does not require his creative activity, then the fact that He is the "Principle of the Universe" cannot be contained in the essence as such, i.e. "it is possible to imagine the knowledge of essence, without imagining the knowledge of its being a principle" which implies that "knowledge of one cannot be identical with knowledge of the other" . . . so that God's knowledge of Himself as creator must be additional to knowledge of his essence, thereby implying plurality within his intellect.'[7]

Since imagination is among the least reliable of guides in philosophy, we should do well to consider only the facts about God and his creation of the Universe, rather than what we may or may not be able to imagine about them. The facts from which we can start are:

6.12.   Creation of the Universe is a free divine act.

6.13.   Since God has no potentialities, not even fully actualized ones, it is logically improper to express his freedom by using an internal modal operator, e.g., 'God *can* either create the Universe or not create it.'
On the contrary, the logically proper expression is:
'It can be that (God create the Universe), or it can be that (God not create the Universe).'

Mindful of these points, we have then to ask what sense can be attached to the claim that God's knowledge of himself as creator is additional to knowledge of his essence. Of course, even if the claim were true, it would threaten God's simplicity only if it imputed potentiality to him. So, the point at issue is not simply whether sense can be made of the 'additional knowledge' claim, but whether such a sense would impute any potentiality to God. If it did not, then the claim could hardly count against the divine simplicity.

To determine the sense in which God's knowledge of himself as creator would be additional to knowledge of his essence we need to ask, 'Additional as compared with *what*?' Now, the answer cannot be,

> 'Additional as compared with what God would know if he were *able* to know himself without knowing himself as creator.'

This is untenable not merely because God has never been a non-creator but, even more importantly, because it depends on conceiving him as having an

7. R. Burns, "The Divine Simplicity in St. Thomas," *Religious Studies* 25 (1989): 283.

ability, namely, an ability to know himself but not as a creator. In so doing, it conceives of God in terms that are entirely antithetical to his simplicity, namely, in terms of propositions in which the modal operators are internal. If the divine simplicity is to be respected, however, the propositions used in the comparison have to be ones in which any modal operators are external.

We now find ourselves listing possibilities similar to those in replies to the two previous objections:

> Possibly (God knows his own essence but not himself as creator)
> Possibly (God knows both his own essence and himself as creator of U_a)
> Possibly (God knows both his own essence and himself as creator of U_1)
> Possibly (God knows both his own essence and himself as creator of U_2)

Purely for the sake of argument, let us suppose that what God knows in the first case is less than he knows in the others. In that particular sense, therefore, his knowledge of himself as creator could be regarded as 'additional' to knowledge of his essence. It would, however, be a perfectly benign sense of 'additional,' for the modality is external and hence imputes no potentiality to God. It is therefore quite consistent with God's being simple.

Burns objected that, 'if God's "essence" does not require his creative activity,' then his knowledge of himself as creator must be additional to knowledge of his essence, and that in turn implies 'plurality within his intellect.' But, how could it be thought to imply plurality within his intellect? Only if the difference in modality between the contingency of his knowing himself as Principle of the Universe and the necessity of knowing his essence were thought to require two corresponding *knowings,* one contingent and the other necessary. Since, however, replies to earlier objections have exposed the fallacy in that kind of reasoning, the divine simplicity survives the present objection. It could have succeeded only by showing that the contingency in question imputed some potentiality to a simple God. This it has singularly failed to do: there is no lacuna in God's knowledge.

II. Divine Willing

Freedom — but No Choice — in a Simple God

Because God's creation of the Universe is commonly regarded as an exercise of divine freedom, it immediately prompts two questions for the defenders of divine simplicity. One is, how can God's willing to create the Universe be free if he is devoid of all abilities, for surely he must have at least one ability, namely, the ability to choose what to do? The other question is, how can his willing to create the Universe be free if his simplicity precludes his having more than one willing? Let us consider these in turn.

The doubt as to whether God can reasonably be said to lack all potentiality arises because, if he is free to will to create the Universe and free not to will it, there might seem to be obvious grounds for saying that he is *able* to will it or not to will it. Now, if we ourselves were faced with such choices there would be a moment when we would consider the alternatives, at which point we would be merely *capable* of opting for either one of them. There would then be a subsequent moment when, being attracted by the superior merits of one, we would in fact choose it. Not so, however, with a simple God; for an entity whose existence is devoid of all bounds could never at any moment be merely *capable* of opting for one of the alternatives, a moment in which he weighed them all up, before being so attracted by the merits of one as *actually* to choose it.[8] To maintain that there really could be such a moment would, in effect, be to conceive of God both as *lacking* all potentiality (because zero-bounded) and as *not* lacking all potentiality, because having the potentiality to choose one among various options.

So much the worse for a simple God, thinks Keith Ward, who makes his point with admirable clarity:

... if the world is contingent, then it could have been otherwise. And if it could have been otherwise, then God could have created a different world from the one he actually did create. One can only understand that 'could have' as an admission that there are at least some unrealised possibilities in God—namely, the creation of those beings which he did not create, though he could have done so.[9]

As we shall see, however, this confident claim rather begs the question.

In concluding that 'there are some unrealized possibilities in God,' Ward apparently supposes the logical role of 'could have' in such propositions as 'God could have created a different world from the one he actually did create' is that of an internal operator. He seems to have ignored the possibility of 'could have' being used externally as in 'It could have been that (God create a

---

8. '... if there is no potentiality in the divine will, God does not thus prefer one of the opposites among his effects as if he should be thought of as being in potency to both, so that he first wills both in potency and afterwards he wills in act. Rather, he wills in act whatever he wills' (Aquinas, *Summa contra Gentiles*, Bk.I, c.82 [7]).

9. K. Ward, *The Concept of God* (Oxford: Blackwell, 1974), 157.

different world from the one he actually does create).' Which use, then, is correct in the present case, the internal or the external? If God is simple, it will be the external use; if he is not simple, it will be the internal one. To justify Ward's internal use, therefore, he had *already* to have known that God was not simple. In other words, he had to know precisely what he purports to be proving. So, his objection turns out to be question-begging.

The external use of the possibility operator is important to the defender of divine simplicity not in establishing that God has no potentialities—for that has been achieved by other means—but merely in explaining one of the ways in which language about a simple God must differ from language about a God that was endowed with some potentiality. The external use of 'could have' is mandatory in talk about a simple God since it imputes no potentiality to him and thus is perfectly consistent with there being not even a logical moment, let alone a temporal one, when God could properly be depicted as conforming to the so-called 'standard picture of divine agency,'[10] namely, as surveying the range of options open to him prior, logically, to choosing to create the actual universe U_a. That is to say, the external use of 'could have' is consistent with the creation of U_a not being *chosen* by God, but simply being *willed* by him. Although he does not *choose* to create U_a, he does *will* to do so. *Choice* is alien to God because it entails potentiality, but *willing* is not. And, because it is not necessary that he will to create, his willing is entirely free, notwithstanding the absence of choice.[11]

The second of the questions I mentioned above is prompted by the contrast between the necessity of God's willing his own goodness and the contingency of his willing to create U_a. The suggestion is that, since different modalities are involved here, there should also be different willings, one of which is necessary and the other free. Thus, in *The Mind of God*, Paul Davies is much exercised by the 'serious difficulties relating this timeless, necessary being [God] to the changing, contingent world of experience.'[12] Quoting approvingly from Keith Ward, he notes that 'if God is the creator or cause of a

10. The phrase is from P. Grim's review of J. Tomberlin, ed., *Philosophical Perspectives* 5 (1991). Cf. *Nous* 28 (1994): 405–14.

11. Two years after reaching this conclusion I read Grim's review in the 1991 volume of *Philosophical Perspectives* in which he drew attention to four arguments on quite disparate topics in the volume which 'together seem to be telling us that there is something quite fundamentally wrong with the standard picture of divine agency' (p. 411). 'What is called for,' he claimed, 'is an abandonment of crucial elements of the standard picture' (p. 413). He suggested that one of the elements to be abandoned might be that of 'deliberate choice.' Indeed it might.

12. P. Davies, *The Mind of God* (New York: Simon and Schuster, 1992), 191.

contingent world, he must be contingent and temporal; but if God is a necessary being, then whatever he causes must be necessarily and changelessly
caused.'[13] But, how can he be both? It is considerations such as these that led
Schubert Ogden to conclude that 'we at once find ourselves in the hopeless
contradiction of a wholly necessary creation of a wholly contingent world.'[14]
To resolve this apparent dilemma, Davies and Ward are drawn towards the
kind of God espoused by process theologians, the 'dipolar' God, who is both
temporal and atemporal, both necessary and contingent.[15]

These questionings—and the desperate responses they have engendered—
might be compelling if internal operators were appropriate in the expressions
of God's willings. They have no credibility, however, given that the operators
have to be external. Why? Because that means that the various possibilities
have to be expressed as follows.

> Possibly (God wills both his own goodness and not to create
>   any universe)
> Possibly (God wills both his own goodness and to create U_a)
> Possibly (God wills both his own goodness and to create U_1)
> Possibly (God wills both his own goodness and to create U_2)
>
> .
> .
>
> Possibly (God wills both his own goodness and to create U_n)

The necessity of God's willing his own goodness requires merely that his own
goodness be an object of the divine willing in *all* the foregoing possibilities.
Similarly, the contingency of his willing to create U_a requires merely that creation of U_a feature in *less than all* those possibilities. Obviously, both requirements are satisfied by the second of the listed possibilities. Note, however, that
it does not require two willings, as the objection suggests it should. Rather, it
contains two objects of the one willing, one of which features in *all* the possibilities and the other in only one of them.

Creating Adds Nothing to God: It Is Merely a Cambridge Property

Newcomers to the writings of Aquinas are often taken aback by his claim that,
although the relation of creatures to God is a real one, the converse is not
true,[16] for the relation of God to creatures is merely what he calls a relation

---

13. K. Ward, *Rational Theology and the Creativity of God* (Oxford: Blackwell, 1982), 3.
14. S. Ogden, *The Reality of God* (London: SCM Press, 1967), 17.
15. K. Ward, *Rational Theology*, 230.
16. *Summa Theologica*, I, q.13, a.7c.

'secundum rationem,' and which I have called a Cambridge relation. Of course, there is nothing strange about a relation being real in one direction but not in the other, for that is precisely the case with the relation between observer and observed. The observer-observed relation is a real one, whereas the observed-observer is not. Mutatis mutandis, the same can be said in regard to properties: the property of observing is real, but that of being observed is merely a Cambridge one. What is so arresting about Aquinas' view is that the asymmetry between being observed and observing is said to obtain between creating and being created, and that the property of creating is said to be no more real than that of being observed (or being spoken of). Yet, such is the unavoidable consequence of the simplicity doctrine. But is it true?

I take up this topic now not simply for its intrinsic interest, but also because it lies at the root of a problem that Tom Morris regards as effectively undermining the simplicity doctrine, namely, the problem of modal uniformity. According to Morris, if all God's properties are identical with him, then either all are necessary or all are contingent: there must be modal uniformity among them.[17] But his omnipotence is a necessary property whereas his being the creator of the Universe and his being the caller of Abram are contingent, which critics claim is just what they ought not to be if the simplicity doctrine were correct and all God's properties were identical with each other. Consequently, that doctrine must be abandoned.

The first thing to note in reply is that, in claiming God to be identical with each of his real properties, the simplicity doctrine makes no such claim in respect of his Cambridge properties.[18] For the objection to succeed, therefore, it would have to maintain that both his being creator of the Universe and his being the caller of Abram are *real* properties, properties that make a real difference to him. So, the issue turns on whether God's being creator of the Universe and his being the caller of Abram make any real difference to him. If they do not, they are merely Cambridge properties,[19] and there is no reason to think that they should be modally uniform with God's real properties.

The second thing to note is that Morris' objection could have no force

17. T. Morris, *Anselmian Explorations* (Notre Dame: University of Notre Dame Press, 1987), 109. Likewise R. Burns: 'if He wills something He need not will, then there are still contingent aspects of His being in addition to necessary ones, . . . so that He cannot be absolutely simple.' "The Divine Simplicity in St.Thomas," *Religious Studies* 25 (1989): 281.

18. For the notion of a Cambridge property, see chapter 2, n. 3.

19. Thus, Aquinas maintains that, although the relation of a creature to God is a real one, the relation from God to the creature is not. ' . . . in all things that are referred the one to the other, the one depending on the other but not conversely, there is a real relation in the one that is dependent, and in the other there is a logical relation, as in the case of knowledge and the thing known' (Aquinas, *Quaestiones Disputatae de Potentia*, q.3, a.3c.).

unless it recognized that, in locutions about a simple God, the modal operators 'necessarily' and 'contingently' have always to be used externally, e.g., 'Necessarily (God is omnipotent)' and not 'God is necessarily omnipotent.' Assuming that the objection really does respect that distinction and does acknowledge that only external modality can be operative in respect of God and his attributes, I have formulated it as follows:

> It is necessary that God be omnipotent, but contingent that he create the Universe.
>
> According to the simplicity doctrine, God is identical with each of his real attributes.
>
> Therefore, necessarily (God = his omnipotence) and contingently (God = his creating the Universe).
>
> But, since God's omnipotence is also supposed to be identical with his creating the Universe, then necessarily (God = his creating the Universe) and contingently (God = his omnipotence).
>
> But, both such claims are false.
>
> Therefore God is not simple.

In this argument it is the claim 'Contingently (God = his creating the Universe)' that calls for closest scrutiny. The point of the scrutiny is not to question the contingency of God's creating the Universe but simply to show that the simplicity doctrine is by no means committed to what the objection supposes, namely, to God's being identical with his creating the Universe. My argument is basically as follows:

> God's creating the Universe simply *is* his willing to create it.
>
> But, God's willing to create the Universe is merely one of his Cambridge properties.
>
> Therefore, God's creating the Universe is merely one of his Cambridge properties.
>
> But, the simplicity doctrine does not apply to God's Cambridge properties.
>
> But, Morris' modal uniformity objection tacitly assumes that the simplicity doctrine does apply to God's creating the Universe.
>
> Therefore, Morris' modal uniformity objection fails to undermine the simplicity doctrine.

In support of this argument, I note the necessity of God's willing his own goodness, and that he can will to create the Universe only if he wills *both* his own goodness and to create the Universe. This is quite compatible with the simplicity doctrine because, although multiple objects of God's willing are consistent with God's being simple, multiple divine willings are not. We need now to determine just how God's own goodness and creation of the Universe are related as objects of the one divine willing. To do so, we need first to consider some of the ways in which two items might be willed in the one willing, and then to determine whether any one of them would be appropriate to a God who is simple. Three such ways are illustrated below:

6.14. Mary wills to give her two daughters, Rachel and Allison, separate reprimands.

6.15. Mary wills that Rachel go to the bus stop to bring Allison home.

6.16. Mary wills her brother Tom's good, but wills the good of Susan *solely* qua being Tom's daughter. Note that Mary need not be willing Susan's good in order to *please* Tom, for he may be completely oblivious of her feelings towards his daughter. Note also that Mary does not have two grounds for willing Susan's good, namely, both in her own right and qua Tom's daughter. Rather, she has no reason at all to will Susan's good in her own right but finds her utterly repulsive.

In (6.14), although two reprimands are willed in the one act of willing neither is in any way subordinate to the other. It therefore differs from (6.15), in which Rachel's going to the bus stop is willed as subordinate to bringing Allison home, i.e., as a *means* to that end. Neither case, however, illustrates how God wills both his own goodness and the creation of the Universe; and I have mentioned them merely to preclude the third case from being confused with either of the first two. Case (6.14) is unhelpful, since it would imply that creation of the Universe was willed in its own right, and that if God had not created the Universe he would have lacked something, and thus have been bounded in some way. Case (6.15) is unhelpful, because it would imply that God's willing his own goodness was in some way dependent on his willing to create the Universe. In other words, the supreme good would not be God *tout court*, but only God as creating the Universe: creation of the Universe would be a contingent addition to God's essential goodness.

As depicted in (6.16), Mary's willing is a far better analogue of the divine willing than those in the first two cases. Mary is not willing Susan's good because of anything at all attractive about Susan. Had she been doing so, then her willing Tom's good *and* Susan's good would have been different from her willing Tom's good alone: in this respect, therefore, it would have been like her willing to reprimand both Rachel and Allison. Nor is she willing Susan's good as a *means* of willing Tom's good,[20] as in the second case. Rather, she is willing it purely and simply as an expression of her goodwill towards Tom. Since she wills Susan's good solely qua willing Tom's, there is no difference, either numerically or qualitatively, between her goodwill towards Susan and her goodwill towards Tom alone. In this case, although Mary's goodwill towards Susan may make a difference to *Susan*, it makes no difference to Mary's goodwill towards Tom. Of course, I am not saying it makes no difference to what Mary may *do*. My point is merely that, no matter how she may act towards Susan, it does not indicate any variation in her goodwill towards Tom, but is simply another way of expressing that same goodwill.

Since there are doubtless many disanalogies between Mary's goodwill towards Susan and God's willing to create the Universe, let me stress as strongly as I possibly can that I am using the analogy to illustrate *one point, and one point only*. That point, in the case as I have described it, is that variations in regard to the *number of objects* of Mary's goodwill entail no variation at all in the *goodwill itself*. The goodwill would have been unchanged even had Tom been plagued by ten utterly repulsive offspring, each of whose good Mary willed solely qua their being his children.

So far as the comparison between God's willing to create the Universe and Mary's loving Susan is concerned, the *one and only* similarity on which I rely is that creation is something God wills not *in its own right*, but *solely* qua being a manifestation of his own goodness. Thus, from God's point of view, the Universe has nothing to commend it except to the extent that it is a manifestation of his own goodness.[21] Just as Mary's goodwill towards Tom *and* Susan neither adds to nor detracts from her goodwill towards Tom alone, so likewise God's willing both his own goodness *and* creation of the Universe neither adds to nor detracts from his willing of his own goodness alone. Such a willing is no more affected by the number of items falling under its umbrella than was Mary's goodwill affected by the number of Tom's utterly unlovable children. Even though the Universe's falling under the umbrella of God's willing his own goodness makes a great difference to the Universe, it makes simply no difference to God's willing. But, if willing to create the Universe makes no difference to God's willing, it can be no more than a Cambridge property of him. And, so far as the simplicity doctrine is con-

20. Of course, Susan's good does contribute to Tom's, but the point is that Mary's *goodwill* towards Susan neither adds to nor subtracts from her goodwill towards Tom, since the former is nothing other than the latter.

21. That does not mean that the Universe could be as repulsive as Susan. On the contrary, to the extent that it manifests God's goodness, it itself is also good in many respects.

cerned, it is therefore quite irrelevant whether it be modally uniform with God's omnipotence or not.

Even if *willing* to create the Universe is not something that God does over and above simply being God (and hence willing his own goodness), it might nevertheless be urged that the act of creation—the *implementing* of what he wills—is surely something over and above his simply being God. Consequently, even if he had not created the Universe, he would nevertheless have had the potentiality to do so, in which case he could not be simple. Certainly, if God's actions were like ours, that claim would be undeniable. In human actions, we have not only to will to do something, we have also to do it: we may have to set to work on various materials to produce our desired result. In creation, however, God has nothing to work on,[22] and so there is no question of his rolling up the divine sleeves to create the Universe. To create it, he has only to will it: his willing it *is* his doing it. So, his actually creating the Universe is not something over and above his willing to create it. And, since the latter is only a Cambridge property of God, so too is the former.

For two reasons it has been crucial to understand that a simple God wills to create the Universe only qua manifesting his own goodness. First, and obviously, it removes any temptation to think there are *two* willings, one a willing of the divine goodness and the other a willing to create the Universe. On the contrary, there is only one. Second, and less obviously, it removes any temptation to think that there is some *intrinsic* difference between God's willing his own goodness *alone* on the one hand and his willing *both* his own goodness and to create the Universe on the other hand. As we have seen, this makes a difference to the Universe, but no *intrinsic* difference to God.[23] So, Aquinas was right.

The upshot for Morris' objection is clear enough. He argued that, since

22. As I argue in chapter 7, that is true even *subsequent* to his creating the Universe, the reason being that God does not act *on* the Universe even then. He does not cause the Universe to continue in existence but, rather, causes it to be that (the Universe continue in existence). Once again, it is crucial to distinguish these two kinds of logical construction.

23. Aquinas makes a similar point: 'Creation signified actively means the divine action, which is God's essence with a relation to the creature. But in God relation to the creature is not a real relation, but only a relation of reason; whereas the relation of the creature to God is a real relation' (*Summa Theologica*, I, q.45, a.3, ad 1um). Nor should it be thought that such a mammoth effect as the existence of the Universe could have been achieved only with a correspondingly mammoth expenditure of divine 'energy.' Energy is required in human productions in order to overcome the resistance of materials to being moulded according to the human will. Since a creator God has no materials to contend with, nor anyone who could thwart him, the question of his expending energy does not arise.

God's omnipotence was a necessary property and his creating the Universe was contingent one, God could not be simple. However, since the divine simplicity holds merely for God's real properties, the objection would be cogent only if God's omnipotence and his creating the Universe were *both* real properties. Because his creating the Universe has now turned out to be merely a Cambridge property, the objection must lapse.

Conclusion

This chapter defended the simplicity doctrine against what seemed initially to be some quite cogent objections. Moreover, in the course of doing so, it produced some invaluable spin-offs. It was telling evidence of how difficult it seems to be for even good scholars to grasp what it means to say that God really is devoid of all potentiality, even of potentiality that is fully exercised. The objections of Morris, Leftow, Burns, and Ward each witnessed to the unhappy consequences of not realizing that this means that modal operators can be used only externally in talk about a God who lacks all potentiality.

Some of the implications of that lack of potentiality have surfaced in the chapter. For one thing, it has meant that, although such a God knows all things, there cannot be multiple acts of divine cognition. What there can be is one act in which God knows himself and, in so doing, knows everything being caused by him. Nor can there be multiple divine acts of willing. What there can be is one act in which God wills his own goodness and, in so doing, wills everything else precisely as manifesting that goodness.

A second implication of God's lack of potentiality is that it does not preclude some truths about him from being contingent: lack of potentiality is not to be equated with lack of contingency. There can be no contradiction between 'Necessarily (God knows himself)' and 'Contingently (God knows the Universe)', for all that means is that God knows himself in all possible worlds and knows the Universe in less than all possible worlds. Had it been possible for the modal operators to be internal—as in 'God necessarily knows himself' and 'God contingently knows the Universe'—there would indeed have been a problem, for the latter does imply potentiality in God. Mutatis mutandis, the same points can be made about God's willing.

A third implication of lack of potentiality in God is that, although the relation of creatures to him is real, the relation of him to creatures is only a Cambridge relation. Even though being created is a real property of creatures, creating is not a real property of God. And a fourth implication has been that God makes no choices—even though he is indeed endowed with free will.

Besides the objections in this chapter, there are a number considered in its Appendix, each of which is evidence of the difficulties that arise from failing to recognize that God's properties are not mere extensions of human ones but are in fact their limit cases.

Appendix

Further Objections to the Simplicity Doctrine

Failure to recognize that God's properties are not mere extensions of creaturely properties, but are in fact their limit cases, has led to such spurious notions as God's being a property, or having a property, or sharing a property, or exemplifying a property, or having a property instance, or being a property instance. It also spawned a number of objections based on those same misguided notions. Eight of them are discussed and rebutted in this appendix.

Is God Dependent on Properties?

Not only does the identity between God and his existence manifest the richness of Subsistent Existence, his identity with the limit case instances of properties has the additional merit of refuting the following suggestion:

Suppose God has essentially the property of being omnipotent and suppose that property is an object distinct from him, is uncreated by him and exists necessarily. Then in some sense he does depend on that property. For in the first place he could not have existed if it had not. . . . And secondly he couldn't have the character he does have, couldn't be the way he is, if omnipotence didn't exist or weren't the way *it* is.[1]

Since I see no reason at all to think that a property is any kind of object whatever, let alone one that is 'an object distinct from him, is uncreated, and exists necessarily,' I am unmoved by this objection. But, even if I were wrong and a property really were such an object, the objection would still have no force, for it rests on the false presupposition that God would *exemplify* that property. The fact is, however, that this is just what a simple God would not

---

1. A. Plantinga, *Does God Have a Nature?* (Milwaukee: Marquette University Press, 1980), 34. Richard Gale raises much the same objection in his *On the Nature and Existence of God* (Cambridge: Cambridge University Press, 1991), 25.

do; for his omnipotence is the *limit case* instance of being powerful, and hence is not an instance or exemplification of being powerful nor indeed of any other property either. Consequently, even if properties really did belong to a 'Platonic menagerie,' there is no sense whatever in which God would depend on them. Nor, of course, does he depend even on their limit case instances, the simple reason being that he does not exemplify them but is identical with them.

Is God a Property Instance?

This objection assumes that the claim 'God is his property *F*' entails that God is a property instance. The entailment would hold, however, only if *his* instance of *F* were itself a property instance in a univocal sense of that term. But that has already been shown to be false precisely because he is a *limit case* instance of *F*, and a limit case instance of *F* is not an instance of *F* in any univocal sense.

Simplicity and the Paradox of Perfection

According to Richard Gale, supporters of the simplicity doctrine are logically committed to accepting that even an absolutely perfect being could be less perfect in some respects than a non-perfect being would be. Hence what he calls the 'paradox of perfection' that 'no one is perfect, not even the absolutely perfect being.' He dubs it 'a devastating atheological argument,' and it goes thus:

Let a Pinrod be a possible being who has only one of the divine perfections— omnipotence—and thereby does not qualify as an absolutely perfect being. . . . Not being burdened with being absolutely perfect, our Pinrod, in addition to having all of God's powers, for instance, being able to create a universe ex nihilo and perform other parlor tricks, can be possessed of a body and thereby be able to play football. Since he is not absolutely perfect, he is not barred from committing suicide. Furthermore, since he lacks benevolence, he is able to perform an immoral action. Thus, this lesser being has a greater degree of freedom than that possessed by God, an absolutely perfect being. It looks as if no one is perfect, not even an absolutely perfect being![2]

The paradox could be evaded by showing it to be impossible that any being have one of God's perfections without having them all. At first glance, this

---

2. Gale, *On the Nature and Existence of God*, 23.

might seem to be done quite easily—merely by appealing to the simplicity doctrine's claim that the absolutely perfect being's perfections are identical with each other. The fallacy in this suggestion, says Gale, is its assumption that a token identity proposition entails a type identity proposition. He insists, on the contrary, that the fact that one instance of omnipotence (God's) is identical with one instance of benevolence certainly does not entail that *every* instance of omnipotence will be identical with an instance of benevolence. Consequently, if someone other than God were omnipotent, they need not be benevolent, and hence would have more freedom in the exercise of their omnipotence than God has in the exercise of his.

Whatever may be the case in regard to the simplicity doctrine as framed in terms of instances of perfections—and I do not intend to pursue that point—Gale's argument is irrelevant to the doctrine as framed in terms of *limit case* instances of perfections. The fundamental fallacy in the argument lies in what it ascribes to God, namely, an instance of omnipotence and an instance of benevolence or, more accurately, of omnibenevolence. According to the limit case account of divine simplicity, however, omnipotence is the limit case instance of power, and omnibenevolence is the limit case instance of benevolence. If the objection is to be relevant to a simple God, therefore, Gale's 'an instance of omnipotence' would have to be 'an instance of the limit case instance of omnipotence'; and 'an instance of omnibenevolence' would have to be 'an instance of the limit case instance of benevolence.' Unfortunately, neither of these locutions makes any sense, for limit case instances simply cannot be instantiated: they themselves do not admit of instances. In respect of limit cases, therefore, the distinction between token identity propositions and type identity propositions is simply inadmissible. That distinction, however, was the linchpin in Gale's argument: without it, the 'devastating' atheological argument is anything but devastating.

Can God Have Only One Essential Attribute?

Plantinga has argued that 'if God is identical with each of his properties, then each of his properties is identical with each of his properties, so that God has but one property. This seems flatly incompatible with the obvious fact that God has several properties.'[3] He concludes that, if God is simple, then he is nothing but a property. As it stands, this objection is based on the mistaken view that the simplicity doctrine requires God to be identical with properties

---

3. Plantinga, *Does God Have a Nature?* 47.

as such. It therefore has no purchase against the limit case account of that doctrine. We might, however, consider whether it would be more successful, were it reformulated in terms of limit cases, as follows:

> If God is identical with the limit case instances of properties
> F, G, H, then each of those limit case instances is identical with
> each other, so that God is identical with but one limit case
> instance. This seems flatly incompatible with the fact that God
> has several properties.

The problem seems to be this: how can God be said to have *distinct* properties F, G, H if he is *not distinct* from the limit case instances of those properties, nor they from each other? The answer is simply that, although there is no distinction *in God* between those limit cases, that does not preclude his being denominated *by us* in different ways corresponding to the differences between those properties of which he is the limit case instance. Thus, in view of his being the limit case instance of F, we can speak of him as being F, but since he is also the limit case instance of G, we can also speak of him as being G, and so on for all the other limit cases. Although there is no distinction between the limit cases *in se*, we humans can draw a distinction, albeit one that is based not on any inherent difference between the limit cases *themselves* but simply on the differences between those *properties simpliciter* of which they are the limit case instances.

As for the conclusion that a simple God would be a limit case instance, that is quite correct. Although it would be unacceptable to say that he was either a property simpliciter or a (*non*-limit case) property instance, there is no objection to saying that he is a limit case property instance. It would be a gross misunderstanding of the limit case account of divine simplicity, however, to think that this was in any way demeaning to God. The reason is that the limit case instance of F is not a property instance. In fact, it is no more a property instance than negative growth is growth, for both 'limit case' in 'limit case instance' and 'negative' in 'negative growth' are alienans adjectives.

Can God Have Unique Properties?

Starting from the irreproachable premiss that the F-ness of x and the G-ness of y cannot be identical unless every property exemplified by x's F-ness is exemplified by y's G-ness, Morris concludes that no property that is unique to God could be identical with one that he shares with creatures.[4] He reasons that if God's F-ness were unique to him, it would have the property of being

4. Morris, *Anselmian Explorations*, 117–18.

unique to him; whereas if his *G*-ness were shared with creatures, it would have the property of *not* being unique to him. Since his *F*-ness and his *G*-ness would have different properties, they could not be identical with each other.

This objection suffers from a recurring defect common to virtually all perfect-being theology, namely, of tacitly assuming that the difference between God's real properties and those of creatures is merely one of specific difference or perhaps degree, albeit of an extraordinarily high degree. As a consequence, the perfect-being theologian sees nothing incongruous in speaking of God's *sharing* real properties with creatures. It is a corollary of their view that such predicates as '____ is wise' and '____ is intelligent' would be predicated univocally of both God and creatures. What this assumption overlooks is that God's real property instances are limit case property instances, and thus differ *absolutely* from those had by creatures. Strictly speaking, therefore, although there is at least some similarity between God's properties and those of creatures, God does not *share* any property at all with his creatures—not his wisdom, not his intelligence, not his power, not his knowledge, nor any other real property. Since Morris has assumed that God *does* have shared properties,[5] his objection has no force.

How Can God's Properties Be Co-extensive?

Morris also argues that, if no two property instances can be identical unless the properties they instantiate are co-extensive, God's knowledge and his power cannot be identical.[6] Once again, however, the misconception is in thinking that *God's* instance of knowledge and his instance of power are instances of knowledge and power respectively. The fact that they are *limit case* instances of knowledge and power, however, means that they are *not* instances of knowledge and power in any univocal sense. So it really is irrelevant whether knowledge and power are co-extensive or not, for lack of co-extension between properties does not entail lack of identity between their *limit cases*. For example, although being a regular polygon and being a series of dots arranged in circular form are not co-extensive, their limit cases are identical, viz. being a circle.

How Can Different Properties Be Identical in God?

In an objection not unrelated to the preceding one, Christopher Hughes has argued as follows:

5. Morris goes so far as to claim that it is 'not even coherent' to say that none of God's properties are shared. Cf. ibid., 118.

6. Ibid., 116.

If God's goodness = God's wisdom, then there is no difference
between goodness and wisdom.
But goodness and wisdom do differ.
Therefore, God's goodness cannot be identical with his wisdom.

Stump and Kretzmann[7] had replied to this objection by substituting 'perfect goodness' for 'goodness' and 'perfect wisdom' for 'wisdom,' and by then arguing that 'God's (perfect) goodness = God's (perfect) wisdom' does not imply 'goodness = wisdom.' Hughes, however, has concluded correctly that such a move gains the identity doctrine a merely temporary reprieve. I sketch his reasons below:

6.17. '. . . suppose God's perfect goodness is the same as God. Since God
could not be a property of anything else, neither could God's perfect
goodness. So there is some property—God's perfect goodness—
which is a property of itself (since it is a property of God, and God
is identical to His perfect goodness), and is not a property of anything else. But the idea of a property that is its own and only its
own property certainly looks incoherent.'[8]

6.18. He then argues that the appearance of incoherence is misleading,
for it belies the fact that sense can indeed be made of such a property by adopting an account based on Lewis and Quine, one which
does allow for the identification of an attribute with the being that
has it. 'Hence there is conceptual room for the identification of
God with His wisdom, goodness, power, and so on.'[9]

6.19. But this, he maintains, would save the identity claim only if *all*
God's attributes were of that kind. However, even if some attributes
belong to God and to him alone, goodness and wisdom are not
among them since they can be had by creatures as well as by God.
Nor can this difficulty be overcome by maintaining that it is not
goodness and wisdom that are attributes of God, but perfect goodness and perfect wisdom, attributes which are indeed necessarily
had by God and by him alone. This fails, says Hughes, because 'if
God has the attribute of perfect goodness (or perfect wisdom), then
a fortiori God has the attribute of goodness (or wisdom). (Nothing

---

7. E. Stump and N. Kretzmann, "Absolute Simplicity," *Faith and Philosophy* 12 (1985): 353–81.

8. Hughes, *On a Complex Theory of a Simple God*, 63.

9. Ibid., 67.

can be perfectly good without being good, or perfectly wise without being wise.) And even if the attributes of perfect goodness and perfect wisdom are had by God alone, the attributes of goodness and wisdom are shared by God and creatures.'[10] But, 'If God's goodness is an attribute He shares with creatures, then it cannot be an insular attribute, and thus cannot be identical to God.'[11]

6.20.   The attempt by Stump and Kretzmann to save the identity doctrine is therefore deemed ultimately to have failed. It could be saved, says Hughes, only if the likes of '_____ is good' and '_____ is wise' were predicated *analogically* of God and creatures, a condition which he argues is impossible to fulfil.

6.21.   He therefore concludes: 'I don't think one can effectively block the argument at issue for the nonidentity of God with His perfections by appeal to the idea that nothing can be predicated univocally of God and creatures. Also, as best I can see, there is no other effective way of blocking that argument.'[12]

Central to Hughes' argument is his supposition that if God has perfect goodness, then a fortiori he has goodness. This is not nearly so innocent as it appears, for the force of the argument stems from its tacit and perhaps unwitting assumption that 'perfect' in 'perfect goodness' is *not* an alienans adjective.[13] Until the role of 'perfect' is determined, therefore, judgment on Hughes' argument must be suspended. If perfect goodness were goodness which either had a limit simpliciter or could be increased without ever reaching such a limit, 'perfect' could clearly not be an alienans adjective in 'perfect goodness.' In the present context, however, perfect goodness is being presented as *divine* goodness; and *that* goodness is neither a limit simpliciter nor capable of increase without ever reaching a limit. On the contrary, it is a *limit case* instance of goodness. So, if 'perfect goodness' is to be construed as 'divine goodness,' 'perfect' does indeed function as an alienans adjective, for a limit case instance of goodness is not an instance of goodness. Thus, the objection's premise is false, and Hughes is mistaken in claiming that 'nothing can be perfectly good without being good.' At least, he is wrong so long as he clings to his view that 'good' in 'perfectly good' cannot be analogical with 'good' in 'Socrates is good.'

10. Ibid.
11. Ibid., 68.
12. Ibid., 71.
13. For the notion of an alienans adjective, see chapter 1, n. 4.

In fact, he dismisses the doctrine of analogy because he regards as unsound the only two arguments for that doctrine with which he is acquainted. Whether or not he is right about the unsoundness of those two arguments, he is wrong to think that there are no sound arguments at all for the analogical character of God-talk. Perhaps the simplest one is based on the fact that God's existence and his attributes are limit case instances of the existence and of some of the attributes had, for example, by Socrates. It is one which I present in chapter 8 under the heading *Argument for Analogical God-Talk*, and where I show that, between 'good' said of God and 'good' said of Socrates, there is at least some community of meaning, albeit not one of univocity. And that not only exposes a further flaw in Hughes' argument but, in doing so, confirms the earlier conclusion that God's attributes are indeed identical with each other.

God and Absolute Perfection

Philip Quinn has raised two interesting questions against what he calls 'Anselmian simplicity,' which is the view that 'all divine attributes are implied by the property of being absolutely perfect.'[14] The first question 'involves the inference from the predicate "absolutely perfect" to the existence of a single property of absolute perfection. Why should we suppose that there is any such property?' The second question 'involves the inference from there being a single property of absolute perfection to its simplicity. Why should we grant that absolute perfection is simple rather than complex? Indeed, the wealth of entailments Anselmians attribute to absolute perfection suggests that it is a property endowed with a rich internal complexity.'[15] He comments that both inferences stand in need of more support than Schlesinger, a proponent of Anselmian simplicity, has provided. My point in mentioning them is to show that, although they may or may not pose problems for an Anselmian's account of simplicity, they pose none whatever for a limit case account.[16]

Let us therefore reformulate Quinn's two questions in language that would be relevant to the doctrine of divine simplicity even when it is formulated in *non*-Anselmian terms. As so formulated they would be:

6.22.   Why should we suppose that there is any single property from which the other divine properties could be inferred?

14. P. Quinn in his review of G. Schlesinger, *New Perspectives on Old-Time Religion* (Oxford: Oxford University Press, 1988), in *Nous* 25 (1991): 244.

15. Ibid., 246

16. I say 'Anselmian's account' rather than 'Anselm's account' because it is not clear to me that Anselm would have endorsed some of the views of his latter-day disciples.

6.23.   Even if there were such a single property, why should we suppose
         that it would be simple rather than complex?

Any reply needs to recall that no instance of existence inheres in or is received
by anything at all, e.g., Socrates' existence neither inheres in nor is received by
him. On the contrary, Socrates is the *bound* of his instance of existence, which
means that whatever properties he has are manifestations of his existence. In
other words, they are manifestations of the extent to which his existence is
contracted. Because Subsistent Existence is the limit case instance of existence
it has no bound and, thus, there is no contraction of its 'content.' As I argued
in chapter 3, Subsistent Existence therefore expresses the limit case instances
of any real properties which have a limit case instance that is *zero-bounding*.
Moreover, it expresses them precisely in being identical with them.

   There is now no difficulty in answering our two questions. The answer to
(6.22) is that, because the limit case instance of existence has a zero-bound, it
is indeed a limit case from which the other divine property instances can be
inferred. Again, because it is the zero-bound instance of existence, there can
be no distinction between it and each of the other zero-bound limit cases that
can be inferred from it; and that is the answer to (6.23). Thus, the inferences
that Quinn criticized as being problematic on an Anselmian account turn out
to be quite straightforward on a limit case account of divine simplicity.

Divine Simplicity
and Human Freedom

As I have said more than once, it is precisely *in* causing individuals to exist that God knows them qua individuals rather than as merely a unique co-instantiation of various properties. Likewise, it is precisely in causing the unfree acts of individuals, whether animate or inanimate, that God knows they are occurring in the Universe. But what of the free acts? How can he know which of those are occurring? If by causing them, how could they be free? Yet, if by 'observing' them, his knowledge would be causally dependent on them. But, surely this would be evidence of potentiality or boundedness in the limit case instance of existence who is supposed to be without any bound. So, how could he be simple?

Proposals for handling this problem fall into two main groups:

1. Those arguing that our free acts cannot be caused by anything other than ourselves, not even by God. To maintain human freedom while preserving God's omniscience, therefore, his foreknowledge of our free acts must have some source other than his causal activity.[1]

2. Those arguing that the freedom of our acts is in no way compromised by God's causing that we perform them: nothing—not even our free acts—can escape the causal power of God. On this view, therefore, how he knows our free acts is no different from how he knows our unfree acts.

---

1. Strictly speaking, it makes no sense to speak of divine *fore*knowledge if, as I should argue, God is eternal in the sense of being atemporal rather than merely everlasting. In such a God there could be no temporal difference between his knowing events which for us occur at different times. In deference to common usage, however, I shall use 'foreknowledge,' even though 'knowledge' would be the more appropriate term.

Divine Foreknowledge without Divine Causation

At least three attempts have been made to explain how God can have fore-knowledge of our free acts without however being their sufficient cause, namely, one involving Middle Knowledge (Molinism), one involving quasi Middle Knowledge (quasi-Molinism), and one which I shall call Leftow's Second Option.

Molinism

Consider Peter's denial of Christ. To account for God's knowledge of it, Molina suggests that God knew infallibly the whole range of possible situations in which Peter might feature. Moreover, he knew exactly what Peter would do in each of those situations. In particular, he knew that Peter would deny him in certain specified circumstances, one of which was his being challenged by a serving girl. For our purposes it matters not just *how* God is supposed to have known this.[2] What does matter is that his knowledge of it is supposed to be at least logically *prior* to Peter's existing, and hence at least logically prior also to Peter's finding himself in any situation at all. It has therefore the merit of exempting God from any kind of passivity, since it does not result from the causal influence of anything extrinsic to him, whether it be the influence of Peter or of his denying Christ. It is called Middle Knowledge,[3] and the theory that incorporates it is known as 'Molinism' after its author Luis de Molina (1535–1600).

Why do proponents of middle knowledge regard it as posing no threat to Peter's freedom? Because, prior to any divine causality, God foresees what Peter would do in any situation in which he might find himself. What God

2. Among Molinists, God is said to have known it by what they call his 'supercomprehension,' a power that is uniquely divine and far exceeds anything that could be possessed by creatures.

3. On the topic of Middle Knowledge see, inter alia: R.M.Adams, "Middle Knowledge and the Problem of Evil," *American Philosophical Quarterly* 14 (1977): 109-18; W. Hasker, *God, Time and Knowledge* (Ithaca: Cornell University Press, 1989); L. Zagzebski, *The Dilemma of Freedom and Foreknowledge* (New York: Oxford University Press, 1991); A. J. Freddoso, ed. and trans., *Luis de Molina, On the Divine Foreknowledge* (Ithaca: Cornell University, 1988); W. L. Craig, *The Problem of Divine Foreknowledge and Future Contingents from Aristotle to Suarez* (Leiden: Brill, 1988); T. Rudavsky, ed., *Divine Omniscience and Omnipotence in Medieval Philosophy* (Dordrecht: Reidel, 1985); A. Kenny, *The God of the Philosophers* (Oxford: Oxford University Press, 1979); M. M. Adams and N. Kretzmann, eds. and trans., *Ockham, Predestination, God's Foreknowledge, and Future Contingents* (New York: Appleton-Century-Crofts, 1969); C. J. F. Williams, ed. and trans., *Paul of Venice: Logica Magna, Part I, Fascicule 8* (Oxford: Oxford University Press, 1991).

does is merely to place Peter in the situation in which he will be challenged by a serving girl, and in which without any divine prompting he does deny Christ. If this claim were correct, middle knowledge might plausibly be thought to have achieved the twin goals of exempting Peter's free actions from being determined by God's causality, while at the same time exempting God's knowledge of them from being caused by Peter.

Quasi-Molinism

Molinism has been criticized for requiring that, even prior to God's placing Peter in any situation at all, there be truths as to how he would act in a quite specific situation. This raises the vexed question of how they could be true, since at that point no act would have been performed that would make them true. Brian Leftow has sketched a theory that, although free of the Molinist requirement, is nevertheless like Molinism in exempting God's knowledge from being caused by Peter's actions. For that reason it is called 'quasi-Molinism,' and is proposed as 'one way in which a simple, timeless God might have knowledge of free actions that to us are future.'[4]

How does God have such knowledge? Leftow suggests that it is analogous to our ability to predict, on the basis of a close knowledge of Peter, just what he would do *freely* in some possible situation.[5] Any mistake we humans might make about what he would do is therefore to be explained by the limited nature of our knowledge both of Peter's character and of the circumstances of the case. Since God's knowledge of them is subject to no such limitations, however, there is said to be no reason to expect that he would ever err about what Peter would freely do. In knowing him through and through, God would know unfailingly what Peter would do, no matter what the situation might be.

A more detailed account of how God is supposed to know Peter so comprehensively goes thus:

God knows Adam's nature well enough to know how Adam will freely react to the situation he confronts. By knowing this and knowing what the situation is, God knows its consequences, because He knows how this action *would* affect the world. Thus God knows how these consequences change Adam and the situation Adam faces. Knowing these things, God knows what circumstances Adam faces next and what nature he brings to them, and so God can thus know the next free act Adam does, and the next, and so on. If Adam's action eventually leads to the presence of other free agents, God knows the natures of these agents, by knowing what He has

4. B. Leftow, *Time and Eternity* (Ithaca: Cornell University Press, 1991), 262.
5. Ibid., 259. My emphasis.

contributed to the overall situation and knowing the consequences of prior non-divine actions. Thus God can in this way know the actions of all non-divine free agents [including Peter].[6]

Admitting that the story may be implausible, Leftow insists that it is not obviously impossible, and consequently is quite enough to rebut the charge that God's foreknowledge of human free actions would be causally dependent on those actions. God would know them not by observing them but by knowing the nature of the free agent responsible for them. And he would know that nature not logically subsequent to observing it, but logically prior to his creating the individual that comes to exemplify it.

Leftow's Second Option

Quasi-Molinism has been accused of being at least tinged with determinism, since the situation in which Peter finds himself is one of God's choice deliberately made in the full knowledge of what Peter will do in such circumstances. Leftow's second option purports to carry no such suggestion. In it, history is viewed as akin to a novel that God is writing. A novelist may reach a point where he has to choose between having the hero either do *A* or not do *A*. Leftow's proposal as to what happens at that point goes thus:

There *is* no truth about whether the hero does *A* until the author decides what the truth should be. Nor is there any truth about what the hero *would* do until the author decides *that*. All the same, the author's hand at this juncture may not be wholly free. Certain actions by the hero will "fit" the hero's character, the overall story, and the overall style of the novel as so far developed. . . . while there is no truth about what the characters will or would do until the author creates it, all the same the prior content of the story, in conjunction with the author's aesthetic sense, narrative skill, etc., may favor certain continuations of the tale over others.[7]

Leftow attributes the experience of a character *running away* with the plot to the imperfection not only of the author's self-knowledge but also of what was being built into the novel's characters. Since God's insight, however, would suffer from neither imperfection, it might be plausible to suggest that 'an absolutely perfect comprehension of free agents' natures and circumstances, of his own nature, and of the way the former reflect the latter would permit God to "predict" just what free agents will freely choose to do. Perhaps it is just

6. Ibid., 261. Emphasis in the original.
7. Ibid., 263.

barely possible that God would get all of His "predictions" right and not do so by chance or lucky guess.'[8] It should be noted, moreover, that it is not God who predetermines that a created free agent will do *A* rather than *B*. That matter is settled by the agent himself. Although the theory is admitted to be 'just barely possible,' Leftow regards it as being adequate for his purposes.

Flaws in These Theories

Ingenious as the theories may be, I shall argue that none is tenable. In opposing Molinism, I shall not be relying on any of the well-known criticisms it has evoked over the centuries but shall offer two of my own. The first is that it conceives of God's decision-making as akin to the human way of making decisions. I say this because, logically prior to an agent's actually doing *A*, Molinism requires God to be conceivable as being merely *able* to choose to create either a world in which the agent would do *A* or a world in which the agent would not do *A*. As I argued in chapter 6, the ability to make choices is utterly alien to a God that is the zero-bound instance of existence, and hence any theory that conceives of him as having this or any other ability would be requiring the God who *is* the zero-bound instance of existence to be conceivable as *not* zero-bounded after all. For that reason alone Molinism is unsustainable.

Molinism, however, labours under the added burden of assuming that God could conceive of actual individuals logically prior to their existing. As noted in earlier chapters and in the Appendix to Chapter 3, that is precisely what he could not do: although he might conceive of a *description* that would be satisfied by exactly one individual, he could not conceive of the precise individual who would satisfy it. It might be satisfied by Peter, but equally it might be satisfied by any clone of Peter. In other words, God could conceive of there being exactly one individual that would satisfy the description, but could not conceive of exactly *which* one it would be. Yet, in middle knowledge he is supposed to have not merely the *general* knowledge expressed by '*Who-ever* is the sole person to be *F, G, H* will deny Christ when challenged by a serving girl.' Rather, he is supposed to have the *singular* knowledge expressed by '*Peter* will deny Christ when challenged by a serving girl.' Since the former would be made true by *any* individual who was *F, G, H*, it can hardly be about Peter or any other individual either. Only the latter is about Peter. However, since God could not conceive of Peter logically prior to his existing, a fortiori he could not *then* know anything at all about him, let alone that he would deny Christ when challenged by a serving girl. So, God can have no middle knowledge of Peter, nor indeed of any other individual. And that is my second reason for rejecting Molinism and middle knowledge.

As it stands, quasi-Molinism fares no better than Molinism for it, too, wrongly assumes that, logically prior to his creative act, God can have in mind 'a precise, maximally detailed image of every creature He wishes to create'.[9] Nevertheless, the theory could be amended without loss by claiming that God had this in mind not prior to creation but in the very act of creating; for the very first logical moment at which God could conceive of Peter would be in creating him. Although that would be too late to preserve Molinism, it would not be too late to preserve quasi-Molinism, a theory that need insist not that God's knowledge of Peter's nature be logically prior to Peter's existing but only that it be prior to his knowledge of all Peter's *actions*.

The suggested amendment, however, would do nothing to repair quasi-Molinism's basic defect, which is its tacit assumption of there being a logical moment when God knows merely that Peter *would* deny Christ, without however knowing that Peter actually *does* deny him. According to this anthropomorphic conception of God, therefore, he who is the zero-bound instance of existence could nevertheless quite properly be conceived of as bounded (by lack of knowledge as to whether Peter does deny him).[10] It is an anthropomorphism so central to quasi-Molinism, however, that to abandon it would be to abandon the whole theory. I might add that Leftow's second option fares no better, for its notion of God as 'predicting' what free agents would do is one that shares the very same untenable assumption as quasi-Molinism.

Divine Causation

Common to each of the foregoing theories is their neglect of the possibility of God's foreknowledge being achieved not by the likes of middle knowledge, but precisely *in* his causing everything that happens in the Universe. Perhaps this has been dismissed as being inimical not only to human freedom but also

9. Ibid., 260.

10. Some who employ this anthropomorphic conception of God would be disinclined to accept the notion of him as Subsistent Existence or the zero-bound instance of existence, and would therefore be unimpressed by the present criticism. What might impress them, however, is that their anthropomorphism would commit them to accepting that the God whom they hold to be necessarily omniscient is one whom they allow to be conceived of as *not* omniscient, since there would be a logical moment at which God would be ignorant of whether Peter does or does not deny him.

to creatures having any genuinely causal role in their own activities. It is these fears that must now be addressed before finally considering God's foreknowledge of our free acts. In this section, therefore, I shall be arguing for the following conclusions:

7.01.   If F is an activity of any creature b, then God and God alone brings it about that (b do F).

7.02.   Nevertheless, the effect is not to reduce creatures to being instruments rather than agents; for 'God brings it about that (b do F)' does not imply 'God brings b to do F' or 'God makes b do F.'

7.03.   Nor, even, is the effect to infringe upon any creature's freedom.

God's causal role in creaturely activities is a topic with a long history, one marked by at least four competing claims three of which I shall merely note before arguing for a version of the fourth. *Deism* limits God's causality to that of creating the Universe, which thereafter is able both to continue in existence and to operate without the slightest causal input from its creator. *Mere conservationism* allows God's causality to extend beyond creating the Universe to conserving it as well. Although creatures act and react independently of their creator, they are thought to do so only to the extent that he conserves them in existence. While both deism and mere conservationism deny God any causal role in his creatures' activities, *occasionalism* reverses the roles by denying creatures any causal contribution to their own activities, except the activity of free choice. It is God alone who causes their activities, with the creature being relegated to providing no more than the *occasion* or the circumstances in which God causes them. On this view the impact of a swinging tennis racquet does not produce the ensuing flight of the tennis ball. Instead, it is produced by God on the occasion of the swinging racquet contacting the ball. Unlike deism and mere conservationism, each of which was prompted by the laudable desire to preserve the independence of creatures in the exercise of their causal activities, occasionalism was prompted by the equally laudable desire to protect the sovereignty of God from which the other two theories implicitly derogate.

Concurrentism has sometimes been presented as a via media between these conflicting claims, by insisting that creatures' activities are produced neither solely by God nor solely by creatures, but conjointly and with equal immediacy by both God and creatures. On this view, divine and creaturely causations are complementary, rather than mutually exclusive. Inevitably, so pithy a statement of concurrentism leaves some questions unanswered. In particular, we need yet to know just how God and creatures act in concert:

how are their causations inter-related? Do they act in parallel or in series? If in parallel, which aspect of the effect is to be ascribed to God, and which to the creature?

Some suggest that God and creatures do indeed act in parallel, with God being a universal or general cause and creatures being particular causes. What this means is that 'the fact that the unitary effect is something rather than nothing is traceable primarily to God as a universal cause, whereas the fact that the unitary effect is of one determinate kind rather than another is traceable primarily to the secondary causes.'[11] Lest the ascription to Socrates of some causal activity should seem to detract from God's sovereignty, some concurrentists have been at pains to point out that God does not really need any contribution from Socrates, and could indeed dispense with it altogether. In their view, there are three modes of divine activity and in only one of them is there any place for a causal contribution from Socrates (or any other creature). In the other two modes Socrates would make no causal contribution whatever, and God would raise Socrates' leg without any help at all from him.[12] It is therefore not that God lacks the power to raise the leg by himself, but merely that in some cases he quite freely chooses to share his power with creatures. His sovereignty could be called into question only if the first mode were the sole option open to him.

Common to each of the theories I have mentioned is the assumption both that divine causation of creaturely activities would leave no room for creaturely causation (except perhaps on divine sufferance), and that a creature's causation of its own activities would leave no room for divine causation. This might indeed be true if divine and creaturely causation of creaturely activities were of basically the same kind, and distinguished only by the power at God's disposal being incomparably greater than any that a creature could command. Whether that really is the difference between the two causations is open to question, and would seem to be an obvious starting point for any discussion of their respective roles in creaturely activities.

11. A. J. Freddoso, "God's General Concurrence with Secondary Causes: Pitfalls and Prospects," *American Catholic Philosophical Quarterly* 68 (1994): 150. See also his "God's General Concurrence with Secondary Causes: Why Conservation Is Not Enough," *Philosophical Perspectives* 5 (1991): 553–85. My emphasis.

12. Freddoso, "God's General Concurrence with Secondary Causes," 131–56. In particular note: "God's mode of acting when he concurs with secondary causes must be distinct from any mode of acting in which He produces an effect by Himself, without the cooperation of secondary causes" (145). Note also: "God could produce the effects by Himself in either one of two modes, viz. by creating them *ex nihilo* along with their material causes, or by miraculously educing the relevant forms by Himself from preexisting material causes" (145, n. 25).

The Radical Difference between Divine and Creaturely Causation

To understand God's causation ad extra (i.e., production of external effects) it will be instructive to consider what some wrongly regard as merely one form of that activity, namely, creation. The most obvious feature of the creative act is that it is one in which God produces his effects without acting on anything at all. Another, but less obvious, feature is that the creative act embraces not only the first moment of the Universe but every moment of its existence as well. The reason is that a simple God is atemporal: although his effects are temporal, he himself is not. Hence, although there can be a sequence of creative *effects* stretching back to a first effect or even to infinity, there can be no corresponding sequence of creative *acts*.[13] Indeed, there can be no multiplicity of divine acts at all, whether sequential or not. Rather, what we have is one act, the effect of which encompasses the whole history of the Universe, and in the production of which God does not act *on* anything. At no point in that history, therefore, does it make any sense to speak of God's acting *on* anything, and still less sense to speak of any creature being able to inhibit, restrict, blunt, or otherwise affect the outcome of the divine causal activity.

It is in the last-mentioned respect, however, that creaturely causation differs strikingly from God's, for there is in principle no created agent whose effects might not be inhibited, restricted, blunted, or otherwise affected by some creature or part thereof. Thus, Socrates' leg might be so damaged that it could scarcely be raised at all, notwithstanding Socrates' best efforts to do so. Whereas God cannot operate *on* anything, creatures can operate only if they do operate on something. For a creature not to operate on anything is for it not to operate at all.

This claim about creatures might be contested on the grounds that, in cases like Socrates' raising his leg, there is something strange about saying that the creature (Socrates) acts *on* something. Since I have no wish to take sides on other causal issues, let me therefore say that, in affirming that Socrates does act *on* something (his leg), my interest is in making one point and one point only, namely, that the condition of the leg plays a part in determining the outcome of Socrates' causal activity.

The linguistic correlate to what I have just noted is that the appropriate

13. It has been suggested that although God is the first creator, he might have endowed one or more creatures with the power to create. Although a similar proposal was indeed raised in the Middle Ages and answered in the affirmative by Peter Lombard and in the negative by Aquinas, I shall not pursue it here since it has no bearing on the distinction between external and internal causation. A creator, whether God or not, will always be related to non-creators as an external cause to internal causes.

logical form of propositions expressing causation differs, depending on whether the causation is creaturely or divine. Creaturely causation can properly be expressed in such propositions as 'Socrates caused his leg to rise' or 'Socrates formed the clay into a vase' or ' Socrates wrote on the papyrus.' The logical form of each proposition is such as to indicate just what it is that can influence the outcome of Socrates' causal activity: in regard to the first it would be the condition of his leg, in regard to the second the condition of the clay, and in regard to the third the condition of the papyrus.

Since, however, nothing could affect the outcome of God's causation, it would be quite misleading for the propositions expressing that causation to have the same logical form as those that are appropriate for expressing Socrates' causation. To say, for example, 'God formed the clay into a vase' would be to imply both that God acted on the clay and that the clay could affect for better or for worse the outcome of that action. And to say, 'God caused Socrates to raise his leg' would be to imply both that God acted on Socrates and that Socrates could affect for better or for worse the outcome of God's action. To avoid such false conclusions we need propositions with a logical structure in which God cannot be depicted as acting on anything. Now, that can readily be achieved simply by shifting the causal operator from inside the proposition to outside it, e.g., 'God caused that (the clay form a vase)' and 'God caused that (Socrates raise his leg).'

The foregoing examples remind us that the causal operator is like the negation, modal, and tense operators in admitting of both an internal and an external use:

> *Internal Use:* X causes Socrates to raise his leg, i.e., X operates on Socrates to cause him to raise his leg.
>
> *External Use:* X causes that (Socrates raise his leg), i.e., X brings it about that (Socrates raise his leg).

The crucial difference between the two uses is simply that in the former case X would act on Socrates, which is precisely how a creator God could *never* act. The latter case, however, is consistent with Socrates not being acted *upon* at all, which is precisely how a creator God would *always* act. The internal use of the causal operator is appropriate for expressing creaturely causation.[14] It is, however, entirely inappropriate for expressing divine causation: for that pur-

---

14. Admittedly, the external operator is also appropriate to creaturely causation, but only because the internal use entails the external, e.g., 'Socrates causes his leg to rise' entails 'Socrates causes that (his leg rise).' The reverse entailment, however, does not hold.

pose only the external use will do. For these reasons, I shall call God's causation 'external' and a creature's 'internal.'

Peter Forrest has alerted me to a further feature of the distinction, which is evident if we compare 'God causes that (Socrates raise his leg)' with 'Socrates causes his leg to rise.' It will be noted that the direct effect of God's causation—that Socrates raise his leg—has (Socrates') causation built into it, whereas the direct effect of Socrates' causation—the rising of the leg—has no causation at all built into it. To mark the difference, he calls God's causation 'second order' as contrasted with Socrates,' which he calls 'first-order.' This lends further weight to the fact that the difference between external and internal causation is not merely a matter of God's being vastly or even maximally more powerful than any creature, as some theists would have us believe. On the contrary, the difference is an absolute one, by which I mean not only that no amount of increase in creaturely power could emulate the divine causation, but that God's creative activity cannot emulate any creature's causation either.

An objector, however, might still want to contend that the distinction between external and internal causes is a distinction without a difference. Why? Because, if these really were different kinds of causes, one might have expected their effects to be different also. But there seems to be no difference whatever in some effects, e.g., the boiling of water might be caused by God no less than by a flame. I have two comments, the first being to deny that sameness of effect does imply sameness of cause. The criterion for difference of causes is not any difference in *what* is produced, but a difference in *how* it is produced. My second comment is to deny that the effects of God and the flame are in fact the same. What has been overlooked is that God's causation is creative whereas the flame's is not. The flame produces boiling in water that is already there, whereas God would produce not only the boiling but also the water itself: he would produce the water as boiling. So the distinction between two kinds of causation is certainly not one without a difference.

Not to be denied, the objector might now challenge the parallel between God's causing Socrates' existing and his causing Socrates' existing as himself raising his leg. Although accepting that God had nothing on which to operate in creating Socrates, he might deny that he had nothing on which to operate in causing Socrates' existing as himself raising his leg; for surely he had Socrates on whom to operate. If so, the parallel to which the argument appealed would be misconceived.

The new objection relies on God's activity in creating the Universe being distinct from his activity in sustaining or conserving it. However, although there might have been some distinction had God been a temporal being, there is none at all in the case of a God who is simple and therefore atemporal. As explained earlier, for an atemporal God there is only one act in which he creates the Universe and, in doing so, creates it both at the first and at every other instant of its existence. So, the distinction between God's creating and his sustaining the Universe collapses, and with it the objection that was based on it.

The Relation between Divine and Creaturely Causation

Although it is all very well to affirm an absolute difference between God's causal activity and that of Socrates, we are still left wondering how they can co-exist. The difficulty arises because God is clearly the sufficient cause of Socrates' raising his leg since, in bringing it about that (Socrates raise his leg), God does so not only without any outside help but also without having anything on which to operate. But, if God's causation is sufficient for that effect, surely Socrates must be as causally superfluous as occasionalists claim him to be. Can there be any active role at all for Socrates in the raising of his leg?

The short answer to our question is not an unqualified yes, but in one respect yes, in another respect no. Yes, there is no causal role for Socrates in bringing about Socrates-raising-his-leg. No, there most certainly is a causal role for Socrates in the raising of his leg. Lest this sound like mere hair-splitting, remember that the raising of Socrates' leg is not something reserved to Socrates himself, for a doctor or nurse could do it for him. So, although the leg can be raised without Socrates being the cause, it is tautologically true that *Socrates'* raising of his leg — the raising of his leg by Socrates — cannot occur unless it is done by Socrates himself. Hence, if God brings it about that (Socrates raise his leg), he is bringing about more than the rising of the leg — he is bringing it about that *Socrates* raise it. It is plainly impossible that he exclude Socrates from any causal role in that particular event, for he can bring it about that (Socrates raise his leg), only if it is neither a doctor nor a nurse nor even God, but Socrates who does the raising.

This is not to deny that God is indeed the sufficient cause of Socrates-raising-his-leg. Rather, it merely complements that claim by explaining that, *within* the particular state of affairs of which God is the immediate sufficient cause, it is Socrates who is the immediate sufficient cause of the leg's rising. Both God and Socrates are therefore immediate sufficient causes, though in respect of different effects — God by external causation in causing that (Socrates raise his leg) and Socrates by internal causation in causing the leg to rise. Precisely because the two kinds of causation are not in competition, the divine sovereignty can be defended without disputing the role of Socrates' own causation. On the contrary, far from impugning that causation, a creator God guarantees it.[15] Indeed, in the example considered, God could not bring it about that (Socrates raise his leg) without its being Socrates who does the raising.

This conclusion is also a rejoinder to the suggestion that God contributes the general character of the effect, whereas Socrates contributes its particular character. The difference is, rather, that God does what only he can do, namely, produce an effect *ex nihilo*; and Socrates does what only a creature can do, namely, produce an effect *ex aliquo*. It is the answer, too, to those concurrentists who think that what is accomplished by God and Socrates acting conjointly could in fact have been accomplished by God acting alone, albeit in a different mode. Contrary to that view, there is only one mode of divine causation ad extra, namely, external.

Even an objector who accepted the logic of the foregoing argument might still hesitate to accept its conclusion, for it does seem highly paradoxical to say that a God who brings about Socrates' raising of his leg does so without acting in any way on Socrates himself. Just how can God do *that*? This ought not to be a stumbling block to anyone who can accept with equanimity the notion of creation ex nihilo, though without having even the faintest idea of *how* God does it. How indeed can we understand God's bringing it about that Socrates exist without operating on Socrates or on anything else?

Perhaps the best we can do is to conceive of it in the terms I used in discussing the divine omnipotence, namely, as the *limit case* of a series of productions in which progressively less and less of the product stems from the materials being used and more and more from the power of the manufacturer. The limit case would be that in which no materials at all were used in producing the effect: everything in it would be produced solely by the manufacturer. Although something like this account may be the best we can hope for as a notion of creation and of a creator, it leaves us with a most inadequate idea of *how* God could bring it about that Socrates exist if he acts neither on him nor on anything else. Such an inadequate understanding of *how* God brings it about is, however, no bar to our realizing *that* he does bring it about.

15. This conclusion undermines Philip Quinn's claim that 'if divine volition does more than bringing about contingent existence and also brings about events in nature, . . . then no event-causes in nature can be causes of such events.' Philip Quinn, "Divine Conservation, Secondary Causes, and Occasionalism," in T. V. Morris, ed., *Divine and Human Action* (Ithaca: Cornell University Press, 1988), 71.

Exactly the same point can be made about the alleged incomprehensibility of how God can cause that (Socrates raise his leg) without, however, acting on Socrates or on anything else. I say that it is *exactly* the same point, because God's creativity is operative here no less than at the first moment of Socrates' existing. Although our ignorance of just how God can so operate in the leg case may be rather mortifying, it ought to be no more mortifying nor any less opaque than in the case of God's creating Socrates. In neither case, however, need incomprehension as to *how* it happens stand in the way of our realizing *that* it does happen.

The Role of God as First Cause

The relation between divine and creaturely causation which we have finally been led to recognize is one that reveals how inadequate — even simplistic — were the suggested options that God might be regarded as operating in parallel, or perhaps in series, with creatures. Although neither option was tenable, rejection of the latter might encounter some resistance, since it seems to entail abandoning the common theistic notion of God as the First Cause. Yet, although unable to be a first cause in the sense of being the first member of a series of created causes, God certainly can be its limit case — even of an infinite series — for a limit case cannot be a member of the series of which it is the limit case. And it is precisely qua limit case that God is entitled to be understood as the First Cause.

We can therefore say that the relation of God vis-à-vis a series of creaturely causes terminating in effect E is *not*:

$$\text{God} \rightarrow n \rightarrow m \rightarrow l \rightarrow \dots\dots b \rightarrow a \rightarrow E$$

Rather, it is:

$$\text{God}$$
$$\text{causes it to be}$$
$$\text{that}$$
$$\overbrace{n \rightarrow m \rightarrow l \rightarrow \dots\dots b \rightarrow a \rightarrow E}$$

The relationship is the same, irrespective of whether the series has a first member as depicted above or is backwardly infinite as depicted below:

$$\text{God}$$
$$\text{causes it to be}$$
$$\text{that}$$
$$\overbrace{\dots\dots\dots \rightarrow n \rightarrow m \rightarrow l \rightarrow \dots\dots b \rightarrow a \rightarrow E}$$

Had God been a First Cause in the sense of being the first member in a series of agents each acting on its immediate successor, it might have been argued that each member was manipulating its successor, and that God as the first member was the Grand Manipulator. As the diagrams make clear, however, it makes just no sense to regard creatures as *manipulated* by a God who does not belong to any series of manipulators but stands above them. So, such a God neither renders the causal activity of creatures superfluous nor even manipulates that activity.

Even Free Actions Are Caused by God

It would seem clear enough that, if God does not manipulate the causal activity of creatures, does not encroach on or interfere with creatures' own *causation*, he can hardly be said to manipulate them or to encroach on or to interfere with their *free* causation. Nevertheless, some would disagree by reminding us that no human agent can thwart God's will.[16] Consequently, if human acts are willed by God, they will occur willy-nilly, thus leaving no scope for human freedom. Of these two suggestions, the first — that no human agent can thwart God's will — is uncontentious and can be expressed as follows:

7.04. Necessarily (whatever God wills does happen).
This, however, is sometimes used as grounds for concluding that human acts caused by God cannot be free, a conclusion which would be expressed rather differently:
7.05. Whatever God wills does necessarily happen.

Unfortunately, this shift of the necessity operator from an external use to an internal one is invalid, and the objection that relies on it is therefore quite groundless.

Still, that is not the end of the matter, for the same kind of error as might lead someone to infer (7.05) from (7.04) might also lead them to mount the following argument.

7.06. Necessarily (if God wills that X happen, X does happen).

---

16. P. Davies, *The Mind of God* (New York: Simon & Schuster, 1992), 189. 'You really can't have it both ways. Either God fixes everything, including our own behaviour, in which case free will is an illusion . . . or things happen over which God has no control, or has voluntarily relinquished control.'

7.07. Therefore, if God wills that (Socrates choose to read), then necessarily (Socrates chooses to read).

7.08. But, if necessarily (Socrates chooses to read), his choice is necessary, not free.

7.09. Therefore, if God causes that (Socrates choose to read), Socrates' choice is not free.

Of course, the move from (7.06) to (7.07) is no more acceptable than the earlier move from (7.04) to (7.05) and for the same reason, namely, an invalid shift of the necessity operator from an external use in (7.06) to an internal use in (7.07). The same kind of operator shift occurs also in (7.08), leaving the argument doubly flawed. So, not only does the divine causation pose no threat to the causation that is proper to an unfree agent, neither does it threaten the causation that is proper to a free agent. In no way does it impinge on Socrates' freedom.

It has turned out that God's causation of a creature's activity ensures that it is necessary that (the activity occur). It does not, however, ensure that the activity be a necessary one: it may be necessary, or it may be free. Moreover, even in those cases in which it is necessary, the necessity of its activity is to be attributed *not* to God's causation but to the lack of freedom in the kind of creature that is involved in the activity.

Is God to Blame for Human Evil?

It might now be urged that even the foregoing account of divine causation cannot exempt God from all blame for his creatures' misdoings. Even if he does not cause Socrates to commit a crime, and even if he does leave Socrates' freedom intact, it certainly cannot be denied that he causes that (Socrates commit a crime). Admittedly, it is Socrates who commits the crime, but it is God who brings it about that he commit it. Surely, therefore, God cannot escape being an accessory to the crime, and hence must bear at least some blame for it.

Not so, for all we are entitled to say is 'God causes that (Socrates engage in a certain kind of activity).' Whether or not the activity in question is in fact criminal depends, however, on Socrates' intention. For example, the mere cutting of Plato's throat by Socrates is, in itself, neither morally good nor morally bad: it would be good if Socrates were intending to remove a tumour, bad if he intended to kill Plato, and neither good nor bad if he performed the act while sleepwalking. Socrates' intentions, however, cannot be saddled on

God. Hence, even though God does have some responsibility for Socrates' activity qua physical, he need have none at all for the activity qua moral.

This way of getting God off the moral hook would be fine, provided we could be assured that his willing of Socrates' *activity* really could be divorced from his willing its *criminality*. Obviously, it could be if God were ignorant of Socrates' criminal intent. The fact is, however, that he is fully aware of Socrates' intent. Surely, therefore, the morally responsible course of action would be for him to withhold any causal association with the activity, and thus prevent not only the activity but also the criminality with which Socrates' intention invests it. Surely, God's refusal to adopt such a course would be evidence enough that he really did will the criminality of the activity, no matter how reluctant he may have been to do so.

Presented a little more formally, the objection goes thus:

> In regard to the criminality of Socrates' activity, only two possibilities are open to God. One is that he wills that the criminality occur, the other that he wills that it not occur.
> But he does not will that the criminality *not* occur, otherwise he would not have willed that Socrates indulge in that activity.
> Therefore, he wills that the criminality does occur.

The flaw in the argument resides in the major premiss, which lists only two possible courses that God might follow, whereas it should list three. The third is that God neither will that the criminality occur nor will that it not occur. To be absolved of the charge of willing the criminality, therefore, God had only to adopt either the second or the third of the possibilities.

Other things being equal, the preferred option would have been the second, which positively prevents any criminality, rather than the third, which does nothing to prevent it. Other things were not equal, however, since the second possibility would have done violence to Socrates by depriving him of his freedom. The goal of respecting Socrates' freedom therefore precludes the second option, while leaving the third as still a viable course for a God who cannot will any criminality. These moves are of course recognizably part of the familiar Free Will Defence which has long been part of a theistic reply to the problem of evil. I shall not develop it any further here, for that task has already been discharged with distinction by Alvin Plantinga.[17]

---

17. A. Plantinga, "The Probabilistic Argument from Evil," *Philosophical Studies* 35 (1979): 1–53. Cf. also his reply to R. M. Adams in J. Tomberlin, ed., *Alvin Plantinga* (Dordrecht: Reidel, 1985), 371–82.

God's Foreknowledge of Free Acts

Having established both that Socrates cannot choose to *G* without God's caus-ing *that* he so choose,[18] and that the divine causation does not infringe on his freedom, we can at last address the question of whether God's foreknowledge of our free acts conflicts with his being simple. We have come to see that God has foreknowledge of Socrates' free acts in exactly the same way as of his un-free acts, for he knows both kinds of act precisely *in* causing that they occur. For just that reason his foreknowledge of our free acts should no longer gen-erate any difficulties, since he is not causally dependent on us for knowledge of that kind.

Perhaps, however, this conclusion might seem to be premature, for how could God cause that we choose to *G* if he were unaware of which option most attracts us. And how could he have such knowledge except by deriving it from us? The answer is that God brings it about that (Socrates choose to *G*), and that his foreknowledge depends on nothing more than his knowing what he is bringing about. Thus it is that his knowing that Socrates chooses to *G* freely is knowledge that stems not from being at all dependent on Socrates but solely from his causing that (Socrates choose to *G*), which is the causation proper to a creator. His foreknowledge of free acts would be a difficulty only if his causality were internal, which of course it is not.

To sum up. God knows our free acts in exactly the same way as he knows our unfree ones, namely, in the act of causing whatever he himself does cause. For his part, his foreknowledge involves no divine passivity. For our part, our freedom remains intact, since God's causality scrupulously respects our free-dom to choose to *G*. Indeed, he could no more cause us to *G* necessarily than he could cause us to hear freely or to smell freely.

Divine Foreknowledge and Human Freedom

It might be suggested that, even if human freedom does not conflict with the divine causality of our free acts, it does conflict with the divine *foreknowledge* that is associated with the divine causality. Let us therefore consider what has been described as the 'most powerful' argument for the incompatibility of divine foreknowledge with human freedom. The argument that follows has

---

18. Note what I am *not* saying. I am not saying, 'Socrates cannot choose to *G* without God's causing him to do so, i.e., without God's acting *on* him.' Rather, I am saying that, in bringing it about *that* (Socrates so choose), God is not acting on Socrates at all: God's role in Socrates' choosing to *G* is no more than in Socrates' raising his leg.

been adapted from Freddoso's reconstruction of one presented by Molina.[19]
It begins with two assumptions:

7.10. t_l is a time long before Peter's denial of Christ at t_n.

7.11. p is the proposition 'God foreknows, infallibly and with certainty, that Peter will sin at t_n'; and p is assumed to be true even at t_l.

The argument then proceeds:

7.12.   Given that p is true at t_l, it cannot fail to be true at any moment thereafter.[20]

7.13.   But p entails 'Peter is sinning at t_n'.

7.14.   Therefore, after t_l, 'Peter is sinning at t_n' can never fail to be true.

7.15.   Therefore, after t_l, no agent (neither God nor Peter) can make 'Peter is not sinning at t_n' true. That is to say, Peter's sinning at t_n is not a free act.

Although we might well question assumption (7.11) on the grounds that it is not entitled to use tensing in regard to the knowledge of a God who is atemporal, this would fail to impress those who think that God is not atemporal. Still, there is no need to rely on a contentious objection, since the argument is also at fault in misconceiving the scope of the necessity operator in its conclusion (7.15), which implies the following:

7.16.   After t_l, it is impossible that 'Peter is not sinning at t_n' be true.

But this implies:

7.17.   After t_l, it is impossible that (Peter not sin at t_n).

But, this could preclude Peter's freedom, only if it entailed:

7.18.   After t_l (Peter does not possibly sin at t_n).

Since (7.17) fails to entail (7.18), however, the argument offers us no reason to deny Peter's freedom to sin at t_n, not even if 'God knows, infallibly and cer-

19. The references are to Molina's *Concordia*, Disputation 52, and to A. J. Freddoso, *Luis de Molina: On Divine Foreknowledge* (Ithaca: Cornell University Press, 1988), 56. On page 55 Freddoso lists four principles which are presupposed by the argument. As these are clear enough from the development of the argument, I have not reproduced them here.

20. The necessity here is what Sarah Waterlow has called *RT*-necessity (i.e., relativized-temporalized necessity), and which Freddoso calls *accidental* necessity. It is the necessity of that truth which can no longer be prevented, and is employed not only by Aristotle and many of the mediaevals but also by such contemporaries as Prior and Ryle.

tainly, that Peter will sin at t_n' were true at t_1. So, human freedom is no more threatened by our free acts being foreknown by God than it is by their being caused by him.

Conclusion

The overriding aim of this chapter was to determine how a simple God could have any knowledge of our free acts. Proposals involving Middle Knowledge and the like were found wanting, primarily because in one way or another they imputed potentiality to a God in whom it was impossible that there be any. No such problem had arisen in regard to his knowing our unfree acts, since he could do so precisely in causing them to occur. Prima facie, however, that particular move did not recommend itself as a solution to his knowledge of our free acts for, in presupposing that God causes those acts, it would seem to ensure that they could not be free after all. And, indeed, that would have been quite true, had the difference between divine and creaturely causation been merely one of God's exercising more (even maximally more) power than do creatures.

The first task, therefore, was to establish whether this was the main distinction between them, or whether the difference was rather more basic. In fact, the distinction proved to be an absolute one—between God's causation requiring nothing in which to produce its effect and creaturely causation being impotent to produce any effect in the absence of something in which to produce them. Once that was recognized, it was relatively easy to see how God's causation was related to that of creatures, namely, not as God's causing a creature to *G*, but as God's causing *that* (a creature *G*).

Had the relation been of the former kind, all creatures would have been causally manipulated by God and none would have been free. God's knowledge of free acts would therefore have been quite unproblematic, since there would have been none for him to know. Because the relationship was of the latter kind, however, creatures were neither manipulated nor deprived of their freedom for, although God causes that creaturely activities do occur, he does so without acting *on* any creatures. Although this meant that the problem of God's knowing our free acts was still with us, it meant also that its solution was ready to hand. It allowed us to see just how God could know the free activities of his creatures in exactly the same way as he knows their unfree activities in causing or bringing it about that they occur. Human freedom could therefore co-exist quite happily with divine simplicity—and with the omnipotence and omniscience that it entails.

8

God-Talk about
a Simple God

To have argued for the simplicity of God is to have argued for a God who transcends quite radically any other being, actual or possible. Immediately, however, there is the suggestion that, if God is so transcendent, then a language used in its literal sense to describe creatures could surely not be used literally to describe their Creator. Or, more accurately, it could not be used to say anything *positive* about him: if we wished to use language literally about God, we should be limited to doing so in purely negative terms.[1] I shall be arguing, however, that this is just what is not the case. Rather, it is precisely the simplicity doctrine that underpins the possibility of our using language about God not only literally but positively as well. Admittedly, it precludes the *univocity* of God-talk; but that is far from reducing it to 'a piece of negative or apophatic theology.' It is also confounds Ward's view that 'God cannot be described by men. . . . Concepts of God cannot describe, even analogically.'[2]

One of the more recent and impressive discussions of this topic occurs in James Ross' *Portraying Analogy*, in which we are offered a detailed account of how non-theistic language might be extendable—without anthropomorphism—for use about a transcendent God.[3] It is the merit of this and many other attempts at such an account that their effect may be twofold; for, should the account be accurate, the very fact of showing *how* God-talk is analogical would succeed in showing also *that* it is analogical. Its demerit, if such it be, would lie in apparently treating an answer to the 'that' question as inseparable from an answer to the 'how' question: if there were no way of showing *how*

1. '. . . from first to last the doctrine of divine simplicity is a piece of negative or apophatic theology. . . . its aim is to tell us the set of conclusions about God which are *not* to be drawn.' B. Davies, "The Doctrine of Divine Simplicity," in his (ed.), *Language, Meaning and God* (London: Geoffrey Chapman, 1987), 59. My emphasis.
2. K. Ward, *The Concept of God* (Oxford: Blackwell, 1974), 157.
3. J. Ross, *Portraying Analogy* (Cambridge: Cambridge University Press, 1981).

God-talk was analogical, we might seem precluded from ever saying *that* it was analogical. In this chapter I use the doctrine of the divine simplicity to break any apparent nexus between the two, and to answer the 'that' question independently of the 'how' question, and hence without having to endorse any particular account of analogy, whether it be Ross' or any other.

Proponents of the various accounts have been imbued with a common desire to show how language about a transcendent God can escape the bonds of anthropomorphic discourse without producing a language made vacuous by its failing to interlock with non-theistic discourse.[4] Their goal has been to avoid anthropomorphism without however being committed to the so-called 'linguistic discontinuity thesis,' a thesis which might be formulated as follows:

Predicables said of God (e.g., '____ is wise,' '____ is intelligent') are totally unrelated in meaning to predicables of the same spelling and sound used in ordinary discourse. The former have been described variously as being completely discontinuous with those of ordinary discourse, as having 'broken away from its moorings,' as having 'gone on holiday.'[5]

At first sight such a thesis may well commend itself as the natural conclusion to draw, reluctant though one might be to do so.

Not surprisingly, the discontinuity thesis has its dissenters. Some reject it in part by accepting a discontinuity in regard to the literal uses of language, while denying it in regard to the non-literal, metaphorical, or symbolic uses.[6] Others reject the thesis totally, either because they think there is no call for figurative and extended uses of language, or because they think that language may be so extended as to be applicable even to a transcendent God, without being either non-literal or strained to the point of unintelligibility. Ross, for example, has suggested that the discontinuity exists only for those people

4. As in earlier chapters, I am using 'anthropomorphic' in a wide sense. Strictly speaking, a predicable would be anthropomorphic only if it could properly be predicated of a human being. As I shall be using the term, however, '*F*' is used anthropomorphically in 'God is *F*' only if it is univocal with the '*F*' used in '*a* is *F*', where *a* is any creature, whether human or non-human, animate or inanimate. My excuse for this departure is twofold. First I know of no existing word that could fill that role; and, secondly, very many of the predicables applied to God are ones that do indeed derive from applications to humans.

5. Ross, *Portraying Analogy*, 161–63. As he notes, the linguistic discontinuity thesis 'contends that religious occurrences are fraudulent meaning pretenders, whose pretence is negated by the lack of proper ancestry in meaningful discourse.'

6. P. Tillich, *Systematic Theology* (Chicago: University of Chicago Press, 1951), vol.1, 238–41.

who are 'divorced from the *practice* that God-talk functions to modulate'; for such language is not fully intelligible, 'unless you learn it, and its making sense to you is connected with your having or imagining a use for it to modulate living.' On this view, it would make little sense to those who are 'outsiders to the forms of life, the practices, modulated by religious talking.'[7]

Other accounts have been offered by Ramsey's theory of models and qualifiers[8] and Swinburne's notion of analogy[9] according to which the meaning of a term is extended both by abandoning some of the syntactic rules and by modifying the role of the standard examples in the semantic rules. Finally, there are also the more ancient theories of analogy which attempt to explain the literal but non-anthropomorphic character of God-talk in terms of analogy of proportionality,[10] or analogy of attribution,[11] or both.[12] In this chapter, however, I shall generally be using the term 'analogy' in a less theory-laden way than is often the case. In saying that God-talk is analogical I mean simply that, for some substitutions for 'F,' the sense of '____ is F' as applied to creatures and its sense as applied to God are so related that,

8.01.   its uses in 'God is F' and 'Maria is F' have similar meanings,

8.02.   those uses are in no way univocal, not even partially,

8.03.   but are such that 'God is F' is literally (as opposed to figuratively) true.

The discontinuity thesis would be precluded by the first point, and anthropomorphism by the second. The third point does not deny that some predicables in God-talk may be merely figurative; it does deny that all are.

I shall be rejecting the discontinuity thesis, and shall do so by arguing that many predicables of creature-talk can be extended in a way that does violence neither to their literal character nor to the transcendence of the God of whom they are said. I shall be arguing not only that God-talk is analogical and positive, but also that this is entailed by the divine simplicity which, paradoxically, is the very doctrine that might have seemed least likely to support it.

---

7. Ross, *Portraying Analogy*, 177.

8. I. Ramsey, *Religious Language; Models and Mystery* (London: SCM Press, 1967).

9. R. Swinburne, *The Coherence of Theism* (Oxford: Oxford University Press, 1977), chap. 4.

10. Cajetan, *De Analogia Nominum*.

11. B. Mondin, *The Principle of Analogy in Protestant and Catholic Thought* (The Hague, Nijhoff, 1963).

12. J. F. Anderson, *The Bond of Being* (St. Louis, Herder, 1949), 253.

Why the Divine Simplicity Appears to Be a Problem for God-Talk

As we have seen, a central thesis of divine simplicity is that no real distinction can be drawn between God and his existence, a consequence of which is that there can also be no real distinction between God and his attributes. This has implications not only for the syntax of language about God but for its semantics as well. The syntactical point is that propositions like 'God is *F*' are peculiarly inappropriate, precisely because they are not simple whereas God is. Rather, they are complex in the sense that they contain a name and a predicate which, on the Fregean analysis, are related to each other as a complete expression to an incomplete one. The correlative ontological point is that, if 'God is *F*' were an appropriate way of speaking about God, then he would be conceivable as related to his property of being *F* as a complete entity to an incomplete one. If, in addition, God's property of being *F* were a real property rather than merely a Cambridge one, we might infer from the truth of 'God is *F*' that God could properly be conceived of as *not* being identical with his property of being *F*.

Of course, it would not matter if God were conceived of as not being identical with such of his properties as being popular, obeyed, adored, admired, ridiculed, for they are all Cambridge properties; and the divine simplicity does not demand that God be identical with his Cambridge properties. It does, however, require him to be identical with his *real* properties like his existence, being intelligent, being wise, and being compassionate. Einstein may receive the predicable '____ is intelligent,' Socrates the predicable '____ is wise,' and Albert Schweitzer the predicable '____ is compassionate'; but, *strictly* speaking, it is misleading to predicate any of them of God. This is not because they are somehow unworthy of him, but simply because they are predicables which refer to real properties. For that reason, not even the first-level predicable '____ exists' can strictly speaking be said of God.

A striking consequence of saying that no predicable can strictly be said of God, is that such a God can strictly speaking not even be named, the argument for which conclusion is as follows:

> If there were even one first-level predicable (e.g. '____ is wise') whose gap could not be filled by expression 'NN,' then 'NN' could not be a proper name.
> But, there are such predicables, for no expression that is strictly appropriate for referring to a simple God could fill the gap in '____ is wise.'

Therefore, no expression appropriate to a simple God could be
a proper name, i.e., strictly speaking, there can be no proper
name for a simple God.

The first premiss is making a purely syntactical point rather than a semantical
one. It is not saying that 'NN is wise' should be true, nor even that it should
not be as incongruous as 'Mt. Everest is wise' would be. It is saying simply that
'NN' should be no less a gap-filler for '____ is wise' than 'Mt. Everest' is. The
second premiss is simply a corollary of the previous conclusion that God's
identity with his real properties precludes the predicable '____ is wise' from
being said strictly of him. This point will be still more evident in the Appendix to this chapter, where I argue that the only expressions strictly appropriate to God-talk are propositions that are devoid of all sub-propositional
logical parts.

To have accepted the strict propriety of using a name and first-level predicates of God would have been to accept that there was a distinction to be
drawn between the referent of the name and the attributes to which the predicates refer. We should therefore have had to admit that there was, after all,
a distinction between him and his existence, and between him and his attributes, and thus that he was not absolutely simple. We had a choice—either
to say that God was absolutely simple, or to say that he could have a name
and receive first-level predicates that refer to real rather than to merely
Cambridge properties. What we could not do consistently was to affirm both
these positions together. It is not that we could not name God, though some
superior being could: the fact is that not even God could name God. That
alone, incidentally, is enough to show that God's simplicity bespeaks rather
more than lack of physical parts, for such a lack would itself be no bar to his
being named, e.g., although points lack physical parts, they can readily be
named.

Having reached the foregoing conclusion, let me now stress that I am neither saying nor implying that propositions like 'God exists,' 'God is wise,' and
'God is powerful' are useless, and ought to be abandoned. Rather, I am saying
that, though quite useful, they may also be quite misleading. They are useful
because, no matter whether 'God' be construed as a proper name or as a description, these propositions have a logical form with which we are familiar
from similar talk about creatures. For that reason, and because no alternative
forms of proposition are available to us in our God-talk, they ought certainly
to be retained. In retaining them, however, we need to be conscious that they
are of a form which is appropriate to someone who is not his existence but is

merely characterized by existing, is not his wisdom but is merely characterized by being wise, is not his power but is merely characterized by being powerful. If God *were* none of those attributes, but were merely characterized by them, then 'God exists,' 'God is wise,' and 'God is powerful' might be perfectly appropriate for God-talk also. But, precisely because those propositions contain first-level predicates which refer to real (not Cambridge) properties, they carry the implication that God is characterized in certain ways, and thus is not simple. That is why I call such propositions misleading. So much for the syntactical implications of the divine simplicity.

The semantical point becomes evident merely by comparing what we can say of God with what we can say of Boris Yeltsin, Mt. Everest, or anything else in our experience. 'Boris Yeltsin exists' or 'Mt. Everest exists' is permissible, but never 'Boris Yeltsin *is* his existence' or 'Mt. Everest *is* its existence.' More generally, we can say 'Boris Yeltsin (or Mt. Everest) is F,' but never 'Boris Yeltsin (or Mt. Everest) is its F-ness.' That is why a God that is his existence and is his F-ness is radically different from, or transcendent to, both the Universe and everything in it. As we have seen, it is the difference between a limit case and the members of various series of which it is that limit case.

In calling the difference a radical one, I have meant it to be more than a difference of degree such as between Einstein and a moron, and more even than a difference in kind such as between Einstein and an amoeba. For, despite the enormity of their difference, Einstein and an amoeba do at least belong to the one genus—the genus of cellular being—even though Einstein belongs to by far the higher species. But nothing comparable is true of a God that is identical with his attributes. Because he *is* each of his attributes, whereas an amoeba is not, we cannot say that God and the amoeba, or God and Einstein, or God and anything else belong to the one genus. Hence, as Aquinas pointed out, God cannot be a substance.[13] Tillich, also, said as much in declaring that God is not *a* being.[14] There is literally not one thing or any created attribute from which God and his attributes do not differ in this radi-

---

13. Aquinas, *Summa contra Gentiles*, I, 25. 'A substance is a thing to which it belongs to be not in a subject. The name "thing" takes its origin from the quiddity, just as the name "being" comes from to be. In this way, the definition of substance is understood as that which has a quiddity to which it belongs to be not in another. Now, that is not appropriate to God, for he has no quiddity save his being. In no way, then, is God in the genus of substance.' Cf. also *Summa Theologica*, I, 3, 5, ad 1um.

14. Tillich, *Systematic Theology*, I, part II, IIb, 3b. 'God is being-itself, not *a* being.' Emphasis in the original.

cal fashion.[15] Nor, as we have seen in chapter 5, is the difficulty removed by saying that God is *infinitely* wise, compassionate, intelligent, and so on. For, while that is true, it is (or should be) just another way of saying that his attributes are *limit cases* of instances of those creaturely attributes. For that reason, all attempts to say anything positive about such a God might seem predestined to failure.

Here, then, is a dilemma. If we want to say that God is so different from creatures as to be identical with his existence and with each of his real attributes, not a substance, and not *a* being, we find that the only language available to us is one that is applicable to things that are *not* identical with their existence or with each of their attributes, and *are* substances, *are* beings. Thus, we seem constrained to a silence, which could be broken only under pain of ascribing to God attributes that differ merely in degree from those had by Socrates, Albert Schweitzer, or Einstein. Language about God would therefore seem to be irredeemably vacuous. This particular dilemma would not arise if God-talk were taken to be saying about God something either merely negative, or merely relational, or both, e.g., if 'God is wise' were interpreted either as saying no more than 'God is not wise in the way that human beings are wise,' or as 'God is the cause of wisdom in creatures,' or both.[16] Nor would it arise if all God-talk were either metaphorical or symbolic (although such theories are scarcely uncontentious). It arises only for a God-talk which claims to be not only positive and often non-relational, but is to be taken literally as well.

So the divine transcendence, no less than the divine simplicity, threatens the very possibility of saying about God anything that is positive rather than merely negative, and to be taken literally rather than merely figuratively. The divine transcendence might lead us to think that a literal use of language could never say anything positive and non-relational about God. And the

15. In saying this, I am denying Alston's claim that there is 'a partial overlap of meaning' between terms said of God and those said of creatures. At least, I am denying it insofar as it applies to terms that refer to *real* attributes. The 'partial overlap' or 'partial univocity thesis' that Alston announces he wishes 'to explore and defend' has the unfortunate ontological consequence of treating God as partially anthropomorphic. For more on Alston's views, cf. his "Divine and Human Action" in T. Morris, ed., *Divine and Human Action* (Ithaca: Cornell University Press, 1988), 257-80.

16. Although the few examples that I have given of God-talk are all predications—indeed, they are all predications employing *first*-level predicates—I use them not to suggest that all God-talk must be of this very basic kind, but simply because a grasp of more complex kinds of propositions presupposes a grasp of some atomic propositions, namely, those that enter into what Dummett calls the 'constructional history' of a proposition.

divine simplicity might suggest that the very logical structure, as distinct from the semantics, of language about creatures rendered it totally inapt for God-talk.

Complex Propositions for a Simple God

As explained in the previous section, the doctrine of divine simplicity has sometimes been thought to *preclude* any literal use of logically complex propositions about God. It may now seem incongruous that the present section should argue that the selfsame doctrine is also the ground for saying that they *can* be used literally about him.

Recall the three conditions for a predicable '____ is *F*' to be used analogically in God-talk, in the very broad sense of 'analogically' defined previously:

8.04.   that its uses in 'God is *F*' and 'Maria is *F*' have similar meanings,

8.05.   that their similarity of meaning be not construable as univocity, .and

8.06.   that, if 'God is *F*' and 'Maria if *F*' are both true, then '____ is *F*' is being used literally, not figuratively, in each case.

Considered on their own, conditions (8.04) and (8.05) would establish merely that the uses of '____ is *F*' were neither equivocal nor univocal, but not whether they were literal or non-literal. Hence the need for (8.06). It is precisely (8.06), however, which is the stumbling block. Indeed, many critics[17] dismiss it as quite untenable, as witness the following objection from Nielsen:

> If 'Maria is intelligent' and 'God is intelligent' have even one similarity then at least one characteristic of God's intelligence is the same as one characteristic of Maria's intelligence.
> But in that case the term signifying that characteristic must be univocal.
> Therefore, to the extent that '____ is intelligent' signifies that characteristic it is not analogical but univocal.[18]

17. William Alston, for example, has grouped analogical discourse with the metaphorical and symbolic as forms of *non*-literal discourse. "Divine and Human Action," 280.

18. K. Nielsen, "Talk of God and the Doctrine of Analogy," *The Thomist* 40 (1976): 40. This passage also illustrates the tacit, but common, assumption that no claim for the analogical character of predicates is acceptable unless its defenders can also explain just what is the *pattern* of logical relations to which the predicates conform. As I have said, I hope to show that assumption to be misguided.

Although Nielsen frames his objection in terms of sameness of *character-istics*, it readily admits of being reformulated purely in terms of similarity of *meaning*. It would then run as follows:

> If the predicates in 'Maria is intelligent' and 'God is intelligent'
> have any similarity of meaning, then there is at least one
> respect in which the meaning of the predicate in the former is
> the same as that in the latter.
> But, then, the similarity of meaning must be simply univocity.
> Therefore, to the extent that '____ is intelligent' in the former has
> any similarity of meaning with '____ is intelligent' in the latter,
> it is being used not analogically, but univocally.

In an argument with premises that are redolent of Alston's previously mentioned 'partial univocity thesis,' the second premiss depends on the possibility of inferring from *similarity* of meaning between 'God is intelligent' and 'Maria is intelligent' to some *sameness* of meaning between them. This rather begs the question, for it could be justified only by assuming that similarity of meaning had always to be understood in terms of sameness of meaning, which is precisely the claim that is being contested.

Nielsen has noted the theistic claim to some similarity of meaning between the occurrences of '*F*' in 'God is *F*' and in 'Maria if *F*'. He is puzzled as to how that is possible, without there being some common core of meaning between the two uses. Yet, if there were such a common core, the uses of '*F*' would not be analogical, but either partly or wholly univocal. Not only that, but the effect of thus predicating '*F*' of God would be to apply to him some core predicates having exactly the same senses as when predicated of creatures. The result would be a God conceived of in the image of creatures—an anthropomorphized God. This conclusion could be resisted, he would suggest, only by abandoning all claim to similarity of meaning between the two uses of '*F*' and allowing that the uses were equivocal—in the strong sense of that term, namely, in the sense of being casually ambiguous. To rebut this suggestion I offer the following argument.

Argument for Analogical God-Talk

The argument is based on the fact that God's existence and each of his real attributes are limit case instances of their creaturely counterparts. Now, as I have mentioned ad nauseam, a limit case instance of *F* is not an instance of *F*. Consequently, '*F*' as used for the limit case cannot be univocal with '*F*' as used for the non-limit cases. There are, however, two other possibilities to be considered. One is that the two uses of '*F*' are equivocal in the sense of being casually ambiguous, the other is that they are analogical in the sense of being systematically ambiguous. Which , then, is it?

To say that the two uses were equivocal would be to say, in effect, that there was no likeness whatever between the members of a series and any limit case that it might have. In that case, however, if *a* were the limit case of a series of instances of being *F*, and *b* were the limit case of a series of instances of being *G*, *a* could just as readily have been the limit case of the first series and *b* of the second series. For example, a circle is the limit case of a series of regular polygons and a proposition is the limit case of a series of predicables. Yet, unless there were some likeness between members of the series and their limit cases, it would be just as reasonable to say that a proposition was the limit case of a series of regular polygons and that a circle was the limit case of a series of predicables. Since that is plainly quite unreasonable, there must be at least some likeness between the members of a series and their limit case.

This general point can now be applied to God's attributes, since they are limit cases of instances of some of the attributes had by creatures. Thus, because God's being *F* is the limit case of Maria's being *F*, Tom's being *F*, etc., there is at least some likeness between the former and the latter, and it is precisely in virtue of that likeness that '___ is *F*' in 'God is *F*' and in 'Maria is *F*' enjoy some community of meaning. For '*F*' we can, of course, substitute 'intelligent,' 'wise,' 'powerful,' 'merciful,' and so on, and in each case there will be some community of meaning between those terms as applied to God and as applied to creatures. Clearly, therefore, the two uses are not equivocal in the sense of being casually ambiguous.

We have thus reached the conclusion that, although terms being used literally of God are not being used univocally of him, neither are they being used equivocally. If, however, they are being used literally but neither univocally nor equivocally, their use must be analogical. And the same must be said of any term at all that is both applicable to God and refers to the limit case of instances of *real* properties had by creatures. Obviously, this is not true of terms that refer merely to Cambridge properties had by creatures: they certainly do not have to be used analogically when applied to God.

The pervasive character of analogy in talk about God has been challenged by Swinburne on the grounds that 'if theology is to be informative, it must use analogy very sparingly.'[19] This claim would suggest that, for the most part, we are quite free to use language univocally rather analogically in God-

---

19. R. Swinburne, *The Christian God* (Oxford: Oxford University Press, 1994), 156, n. 3.

talk.[20] Given that God is simple and that his *real* attributes are limit cases of various creaturely attributes, however, that suggestion is ill-founded. Indeed, much as we might wish it were otherwise, there is no way in which the terms referring to these limit cases can be univocal with those referring to the non-limit cases. It is not that one has the option of using univocal terms but is either too ignorant, perverse, or slovenly to do so. Rather, there are simply no terms that could be used univocally in such cases: the only possible alternative to using them analogically would be to use them equivocally. To insist on using analogy very sparingly in God-talk would therefore be to flood our God-talk with equivocal terms, and hence to eviscerate it completely, albeit for no good reason.

What is true about Swinburne's claim is not that analogical God-talk is mostly unnecessary, but merely that it is admittedly not very informative. Lamentable as we may find it, it is a fact with which we have to live. Although not very informative, however, analogical talk is not entirely uninformative, nor is it entirely negative. Most emphatically, however, it is not what the predominant use of univocal language in God-talk simply could not escape being: it is not the depiction of an anthropomorphic God, a pseudo God.

Replies to Previous Difficulties

In the course of the chapter various difficulties have been raised about the possibility of God-talk being analogical. Principally there have been three:

8.07.   Analogical uses of an expression are said to have different but not totally dissimilar senses. However, to say that they have different but not totally dissimilar senses is simply to say that they are partly univocal.[21]

8.08.   For the analogical character of God-talk, there can be no argument that is not so wedded to one or other *particular* theory of analogy as to be unable to survive the demise of the theory.

20. Swinburne has no difficulty in making this assumption because his difficulties with divine simplicity have led him to regard it as entirely dispensable in favour of the doctrine of divine unity. As I have argued in chapter 6, however, his and other objections to the divine simplicity are far from insuperable; and the doctrine remains indispensable for any adequate philosophical understanding of the divine nature.

21. Although this is Nielsen's main objection, it antedates him by many centuries, as witnessed by the following quotation: 'Those masters who deny univocity with their lips really presuppose it' (Scotus, *Reportata Parisiensa*, I.3.I., no.7, quoted by Swinburne in his *Coherence of Theism*, 74).

8.09.   God's transcendence and simplicity preclude there being any likeness whatever between divine and created attributes. Hence, predi-
·cables that refer to those attributes had by creatures could never be
literally true of God, but only in some figurative sense.

If my argument has been correct, all three objections fail. Most tellingly,
they do so precisely because they ignore the implications of divine simplicity.
That doctrine, considered to be an insuperable obstacle to literal but non-
anthropomorphic God-talk, has on the contrary been the key to removing
the obstacles to the possibility of such language. It has done so by recognizing
that God's real attributes are limit case instances of various human attributes.
This means that 'F' said of God cannot be univocal with 'F' said of Maria.
However, it also means that the two uses of 'F' cannot be equivocal either,
since it is no mere fluke that God's F-ness is the limit case of Maria's F-ness
rather than of her G-ness or H-ness. But, to say that senses of 'F' are neither
equivocal nor in any way univocal is simply to say they are analogous. And
that is the answer to difficulty (8.07). Moreover, since this is the conclusion of
a quite general argument—one wedded to no particular form of analogy—it
thereby rebuts the second difficulty also.

Finally, and contrary to the third objection, neither the divine transcendence nor the divine simplicity preclude all likeness between God's attributes
and those of creatures. On the contrary, the limit case account of divine transcendence and simplicity has proved to be quite integral to the case not only
for the possibility of such likeness but for one that is entirely devoid of anthropomorphism. Thus is rejected the discontinuity thesis mentioned at the
beginning of this chapter.

Conclusion

At first sight the implications of divine simplicity might seem to place severe
strain on both the syntactical and semantical categories we use to talk about
God. They strain our syntactical categories by making it clear that no predications about God can fail to be anything but misleading.[22] Even were that
difficulty superable by replacing predications about God with identity propositions (e.g. 'God is identical with his wisdom'), there would still remain the
semantic problem of how the notions they employ could ever be applicable to
a simple God. Indeed, whether for Kantian or non-Kantian reasons, many

---

22. That is to not to say that we cannot refuse to be misled, but only that we are in danger of being misled.

have maintained that they are completely inapplicable to him: it would be futile to talk of God in human categories for the simple reason that he is utterly beyond such categories. In such circumstances, the most we might aspire to would be to say merely what God is not, though it is arguable that we should be unable to say even that.

Since the peculiarly Kantian concerns are more broadly based than mere talk about God, I shall not enter into them here.[23] More particular are the concerns of those who think that the absolute transcendence or otherness of God entails his ineffability. Despite their major differences, negative theologians and perfect-being theologians manage to agree that God could not be anything but ineffable if he were absolutely transcendent. The latter bite the bullet by accepting neither transcendence nor ineffability; negative theologians accept them both. As it has now emerged, however, the merit of the limit case account of divine simplicity has been to show that absolute transcendence does not entail *total* ineffability, for a simple God is absolutely transcendent without being totally ineffable. Although the predicables that are applicable to creatures are not applicable in any *univocal* sense to a God who is simple, and therefore absolutely transcendent, that is far from denying that they can be said of him not only quite literally but positively as well.

Appendix

Simple Propositions for a Simple God

Having remarked that the logical structure of language about creatures makes it less than suitable for talking about the God of classical theism, I want in this appendix to draw attention to propositions having a logical structure that is singularly appropriate for God-talk, namely, propositions with no logical parts whatever.[1] If this seems a bizarre suggestion, the reason may lie in our accepting unquestioningly that propositions must always say something *about*

---

23. However, see page 158 of my *From Existence to God,* where I address them by employing a strategy adopted by Quine and Geach, namely, the use of relative terms and extrapolation.

1. Cf. my "Logically Simple Proposition," *Analysis* 34 (1973–74): 123–28. Here I give no more than the conclusions and some examples from that article.

something—that not only must predications always be propositions, but propositions must always be predications.[2]

The last claim has only to be stated explicitly to be recognized as rather less than tautological, for what suffices to characterize a proposition does not suffice for a predication. To be a proposition it is enough that an expression be a bearer of truth-value; to be a predication, however, an expression has not only to be a bearer of truth-value, but has also to say something *about* something. All predications, of course, must be logically complex, containing at least two logical parts, either subject and predicate, or predicable and higher-level predicate. But what of the converse? Are *all* propositions predications— expressions saying something about something, and hence logically complex? Or, could there not be propositions that merely said something (with a truth-value), though without saying something *about* something? In approaching these questions we might ponder the warning implicit in Waismann's remarks that, 'by growing up in a certain language, by thinking in its semantic and syntactical grooves, we acquire a certain more or less uniform outlook on the world—an outlook we are scarcely aware of until (say) by coming across a language of a totally different structure we are shocked into seeing the oddity of the obvious, or what seemed to be obvious.'[3]

That we may have grown accustomed to think that all propositions must be about something is not sufficient to show either that they are so as a matter of fact, still less as a matter of necessity. I suggest not only that some could well be otherwise, but even that they need not be limited to the more esoteric areas of discourse. A striking example occurs in a novel by Clemens Brentano: 'Grossmutter, da ist eine Maus drin! hört wie es klappert! da ist eine Maus drin.'[4] ('Grandmother, there is a mouse inside! Hark at the rattling [or, at how it rattles]! There is a mouse inside!') Here the 'es,' being neuter, cannot refer back to the feminine 'eine Maus.' Consequently, it cannot be a referring expression, but has to be construed as merely a grammatical filler. Precisely because the proposition 'Es klappert' contains no referring expression, it cannot be said to be *about* anything at all.

---

2. As I am using the term 'predication,' it is simply a tautology to say that a proposition which is about something is a predication. Of course, the predicates are not restricted to being of first-level or even to being simple, as in 'Socrates is wise.' In 'Elephants exist,' for example, the predicate can be of *second*-level, e.g., '$(\exists x)(x\underline{})$.' In 'If Tom hits dogs, he is foolish,' the predicate would be *complex*, 'If $\underline{}$ hits dogs, $\underline{}$ is foolish.' Each of these propositions is no less a predication than is 'Socrates is wise.'

3. F. Waismann, *How I See Philosophy* (London: Macmillan, 1968), 174.

4. *Geschichte vom braven Kasperl und dem schönen Anmerl*, Bern, 46.

The same is true of the Rumanian 'Fulgură,' which is like a number of other propositions in that language in being no more than a verb stem. It contains nothing that might be considered as even a candidate for being a referring expression—no 'es' nor 'it,' nor even the suffix 't' possessed by its Latin counterpart ('Fulgurat'). More importantly, it is only 'Fulgură' as a *whole*— and not some part of it—that signifies in its own right. It is therefore logically simple. It would of course be invalid to infer logical simplicity from grammatical simplicity; but that is not what the argument does. The argument is based not on any lack of grammatical complexity but on the lack of complexity of *logical roles*, as evidenced by there being nothing in the propositions that has any referring role.

Of course, it may be urged that no one of the allegedly simple propositions *has to be* construed as simple, but that all are equally construable as logically complex. I shall not debate the point here, nor need I do so, since for present purposes it matters not whether they be construable as logically complex, provided there is nothing against their being construable also as logically simple. It would not even matter that logically simple propositions may perhaps entail a logically complex one, e.g., 'Es klappert' may entail 'Etwas klappert' ('Something is rattling'). The sole point at issue here is whether the notion of a logically simple proposition is an acceptable one, and acceptable indeed as one that may well be instantiated in quite ordinary creature-talk. Since at least that much has been established in the article to which I alluded, there is no question of the notion being merely an ad hoc device used in a desperate move to overcome a difficulty in regard to God-talk.

Propositions of this kind seem to be the only ones that are entirely appropriate to God-talk about a simple God. Propositions like 'God exists,' or 'God is wise,' or 'God is powerful' are less than appropriate since each of them says something about something, thereby suggesting the presence in God of the very distinctions that he is said to lack. Their inappropriateness need not, however, reduce us to silence; for it could debar us not from saying something, but merely from saying something about something. Now, to say something without saying something *about* something is precisely the function of logically simple propositions; which is why they alone would be *singularly* appropriate to God-talk.

Logically simple propositions that pertain to God do present us with difficulties not because they are simple, but because to *us* they are almost totally uninformative. This is not so with the aforementioned simple propositions of ordinary language, for they can be grasped in their own right, without presupposing a grasp of any non-simple propositions. For example, a grasp of 'Es klappert' presupposes no grasp of the non-simple 'Etwas klappert,' precisely because we have direct experience of those states of affairs which make both of them true. But the simple propositions of God-talk are not made true by anything of which we have such direct experience. On the contrary, our understanding of them presupposes an understanding of certain non-simple propositions which we may arrive at in different ways—either, as I have just done, by reflecting on what kinds of proposition would be appropriate to the God of classical theism, or as the conclusion of an argument for theism such as I developed in *From Existence to God*. In the absence of any such route to them, a simple proposition in God-talk would not be particularly informative to us. Consequently, God-talk could not be limited to simple propositions alone: it would have to admit of logically complex ones as well.[5]

5. As I use it in this appendix, 'complex proposition' is to mean not 'proposition having *propositional* logical parts,' but merely 'proposition having *sub*-propositional logical parts.'

9

A Most Unlikely God

In this book I set out to explore the nature of the God who, I had argued in *From Existence to God*, was the creator of the Universe and who had to be Subsistent Existence, i.e., identical with his existence. I did so conscious of the widespread incredulity evoked by that notion, and conscious also of two widely differing views of God's nature which many have assumed to be the only reasonable options available to us. One was the depressingly pessimistic view that nothing positive could be said about his nature; the other was the unreasonably optimistic view that almost without exception there was no difference in sense between predicables used of God and those used of creatures. Although radically misguided, such views were useful as a background against which to appreciate both the fertility of the simplicity doctrine and the distinctiveness of its implications for the nature of a creator God. So, first a brief reminder of those competing portraits of the divine nature.

One portrait was the product of negative theologians who, dazzled by God's transcendence, confess to being unable to report anything of what he is but only of what he is not. In their view, philosophers are precluded from saying whether God is wise, intelligent, loving, and so on, since there is simply no way of knowing whether such notions were even applicable to him. In particular, although we might properly deny any *distinction* between God and either his existence or his non-existential attributes (whatever they might be), that would not entitle us to affirm any *identity* between them. The reason is simply that, in saying there is no distinction in God, a negative theologian would be claiming merely that the notion of distinction could never be *known* to apply to him. And that is equally to say that the notion of identity could never be known to apply to him either. Sadly, it is also one way in which the simplicity doctrine has been misunderstood—as merely 'a piece of negative or apophatic theology.'[1] It bequeaths us a canvas that is devoid of anything bearing the faintest resemblance to creatures of any kind, whether human or non-human.

---

1. B. Davies, "The Doctrine of Divine Simplicity" in his (ed.), *Language Meaning, and God.* (London: Geoffrey Chapman, 1987), 59.

Perfect-being theologians present us with a strikingly different portrait in their attempt to make the divine transcendence more congenial to our human way of thinking by reinterpreting it as a transcendence merely 'after a fashion,' or in a loose manner of speaking. This is the sense of 'transcendence' in which Socrates' wisdom might be said to transcend a five-year-old's, not in being radically discontinuous with it, but only in being incomparably more highly developed than it. So, too, with the relation between God's attributes and the corresponding human ones: God's would belong to the same continuum as ours, for they would be merely the maxima to which some human attributes might conceivably be extended.

This, of course, is perfectly consistent with an Anselmian's notion of a being-than-which-nothing-greater-can-be-conceived since, in the absence of any further guidance as to just what such a being might be, it would be difficult to resist the conclusion that its properties were merely the *maxima* of certain human properties. Surely, one might think, it is tautologically true that no property could be greater than its maximum. It would be tautologically true, however, only if one were to overlook the possibility of properties having *limit case* instances either in addition to, or rather than, their maxima (limits simpliciter). Yet, because Anselmians seem not to have adverted to the relevance of limit cases, the divine properties depicted in their portrait are recognizably mere extensions of *human* properties, a fact which not even their status as maxima can belie. Moreover, like human properties, their very coexistence would be possible only if each were tempered in some way by the others—justice tempered by mercy, mercy tempered by justice, power tempered by wisdom, and so on. A consequence of that tempering is that many of the properties could be maxima not in any absolute sense at all, but only relative to what is permitted by the exigencies of having to co-exist with other properties. Small wonder therefore that the portrait is so comfortingly familiar and, to some, so compelling as well.

If the Anselmian portrait is comfortingly familiar, it also falls discomfitingly short of being the portrait of a creator God. One reason is that, although the Anselmians are right to think that God is the greatest conceivable being, they are misguided in thinking that their own conception of him fits that description. For one thing, it is doubtful whether some of the human properties they attribute to God do in fact admit of a maximum. For another thing, those that do have a maximum would still be inappropriate for a being than which nothing greater could be conceived, for the *limit cases* of such attributes would lie beyond even their maxima. Indeed, the limit cases would not be encompassed even by properties that had no maxima, but could be increased ad infinitum. Paradoxically, therefore, those who are most beholden to the notion of God as the greatest conceivable being have proved to be the very ones offering us a portrait which is transparently *not* of the greatest conceivable being.

Perhaps nowhere is the paradox more manifest than in the Anselmians claiming their God to be a creator, while at the very same time conceiving of his creative activity as belonging to the very same continuum as human productive activity, and thereby guaranteeing that he cannot be a creator after all. I say this because human productive activity is essentially a production of something from something: without anything *on* which to operate, no such activity can occur. Creation ex nihilo, on the contrary, is productive activity which is possible only if the operation is *not* on anything at all. For just that reason creation cannot belong to the same continuum as human productive activity: it cannot be what the Anselmians claim it to be, a maximum or limit simpliciter. A God whose creative activity was envisaged as a limit simpliciter of human productive activity would therefore be merely a human being writ large, a being perhaps purged of the grosser features of the Greek gods we so like to deride, but no less anthropomorphic for all that, and no less impotent to create anything whatever. As an attempt to spell out the nature of a creator God, the Anselmians' account is a resounding failure.

The portrait of a simple God, of God as Subsistent Existence, contrasts sharply both with the alien void offered by negative theologians and with the profusion of earthbound and mutually limiting properties depicted by Anselmians. It is one that is not so intimidated by the divine transcendence as to attempt to domesticate it by allowing God's attributes to belong to the same continuum as ours. Rather, their radical discontinuity with ours is respected as inviolable, and God is accepted as so far discontinuous with us or any other individuals as not to be an individual at all in any univocal sense of that term. Despite that discontinuity, however, the simplicity account need not despair of speaking positively about God and his attributes, nor need it settle for a putatively perfect being that proves to be made in the image of man. This, in brief, is the response of classical theism, central to which is a creator God who is identical with his existence, a thesis which I have not attempted to establish here, for that was the task of *From Existence to God*. Here, however, I have been content to explain and defend it. It is a thesis in which God's transcendence is rooted firmly in his simplicity, and also in which any attributes ascribed to him must be consistent with that same simplicity. Hence the pivotal import not only of making sense of the simplicity doctrine but of disarming the numerous objections it has evoked.

Making Sense of the Simplicity Doctrine

As for making sense of the doctrine, critics have had immense fun in demonstrating to their own satisfaction just how nonsensical the doctrine really is, and of expressing their conclusions in a variety of derisory ways. They have taken it to be nonsensical enough that God should be identical with his own existence, but nonsensical beyond measure to expand that claim to include God's being identical with each of his attributes.

My response has been first to argue for a metaphysical basis which I take not only to make sense of the simplicity doctrine but also to be true, and second to explain the doctrine in terms of that metaphysics. The metaphysics in question is concerned largely with existence, about which I have argued that it is not a propositional function but a real property of individuals. Moreover, and crucially, it is quite unique among those real properties in being related to individuals not as inhering in them, received by them, or as conferred on them, but as bounded by them. These were the grounds for saying not only that existence is the richest of properties, but that it makes no sense whatever to ask 'What does existence *add* to Socrates?' On the contrary, it makes a great deal of sense to ask 'What *constraints* are there on existence as bounded by Socrates?'

Presupposed by the claims about existence has been the claim that individuals are not even conceivable (either by us or even by God) logically prior to their existing. And presupposed throughout the whole book is a doctrine about property instances,[2] namely, that there are such entities, albeit that they are not complete entities, not 'little substances.'

Drawing upon these doctrines and, most importantly, the distinction between limits simpliciter and limit cases, perfectly good sense can readily be made of four claims that critics of divine simplicity profess to have found so perplexing. Those claims have to be understood as follows:

9.01.   The claim 'God is his existence' is to be understood as:
        'The limit case instance of a *bound* of existence = the limit case instance of existence.'[3]

---

2. However, I did explain in chapter 4, p. 179, that the acceptance of property instances is not indispensable to my argument. Although I do think that there are such (incomplete) entities as property instances, my arguments could equally have been formulated in terms of there being differences of degree between the various exemplifications of existence and other properties.

3. Since a concrete individual is the bound of its existence, (9.01) could be reformulated as 'The limit case instance of a concrete individual = the limit case instance of existence.' Similarly, (9.02) could be reformulated as 'The limit case instance of a concrete individual = the limit case instance of *F*-ness.'

9.02. The claim 'God is identical with his *F*-ness' is to be understood as: 'The limit case instance of a bound of existence = the limit case instance of *F*-ness.'

9.03. The claim 'God's *F*-ness is identical with his *G*-ness' is to be understood as: 'The limit case instance of *F*-ness = the limit case instance of *G*-ness.'

9.04. The claim '*F*-ness is a property had by God' is to be understood as: 'The limit case instance of *F*-ness is had by God because it is zero-bounding.'

To have made sense of the divine simplicity is to have understood not only why God is transcendent without having to be depicted in purely negative terms, but also why he can be depicted in positive terms without derogating from his transcendence. As for the first point, God-talk could not be entirely negative, for to say that an attribute like divine mercy is the limit case of instances of human mercy is not simply to imply that it is *not* human mercy, true though that be. Indeed, were we restricted to the purely negative claim, it would be a matter of indifference whether divine mercy were treated as a limit case instance of mercy or perhaps a limit case polygon, or a limit case predicable. The mere fact that it is not a matter of indifference at all suffices to show that there is at least some likeness between God's mercy and ours. Moreover, even though the likeness is not of any univocal kind—no matter how attenuated—it cannot be dismissed as inconsequential, for a slight knowledge of God is more to be esteemed than a profound knowledge of lesser beings.

As for the second point, the positive God-talk that is sanctioned by the simplicity doctrine poses no threat to his transcendence for, precisely because the likeness between his attributes and ours is merely one between a limit case and non-limit cases, there can be no question of his attributes being conceivable as mere extensions of human ones—not even of human properties that are extended to the maximum degree possible. Having in this way risen above any temptation to construct God in our own image, we came finally to understand him as Pure Actuality (Actus Purus).

Pure Actuality—A Most Unlikely God

Recall that the limit case account of divine simplicity presents us with God as the zero-bound instance of existence, meaning thereby that in him there is no boundedness, no potentiality. To say that he is devoid of all boundedness is, however, only another way of saying that his nature could be characterized as Pure Actuality. Now, there are two ways of understanding Pure Actuality, positively in terms of what it is and negatively in terms of what it is not. We attend to the positive aspect in recognizing that Pure Actuality possesses all the pure perfections. Thus, we may nominate any pure perfections we like — existence, intellection, wisdom, love, power, mercy, justice, understanding, and so on — and Pure Actuality will have them all. It has them, however, not merely as greatly magnified versions of creaturely attributes, but only as their limit cases. And attributes that are strikingly distinct in their *non*-limit cases can be strikingly lacking any distinction between their limit cases. An immediate consequence of the identity of the divine attributes is that they all co-exist without any of the mutual limitations required for the co-existence of some of the *non*-limit cases. For example, although there may be tension between justice and mercy as co-existing in creatures, there can be no such tension, no mutual limitation, between their limit cases co-existing in Pure Actuality.

We attend to the negative aspect of Pure Actuality when we recognize what is excluded from it, namely, all potentiality. We need, however, to be extremely circumspect in spelling out what this means, and to resist the temptation to conceive of Pure Actuality as merely a being with abilities that are never less than fully exercised, capacities that are never less than fully extended, and potentialities that are never less than fully actualized. This view would be tenable only if the *fully* actualizing of a potentiality or ability were to culminate in there being *no* such potentiality or ability. In other words, it would be tenable only if 'fully actualized' in 'fully actualized potentiality' were an alienans adjective like 'rocking' in 'rocking horse.'

However, 'fully actualized' is decidedly not an alienans adjective; for, although 'rocking horse' cannot be rendered as 'horse that is rocking,' 'fully actualized potentiality' *can* be rendered as 'potentiality that is fully actualized,' i.e., as having the form '*A* that is *P*.' Admittedly, phrases of the form '*A* that is *P*' are ambiguous as between '*A and* it is *P*' and '*A if* it is *P*.'[4] For present purposes, however, it matters not whether 'potentiality *and* it is fully actualized' or 'potentiality *if* it is fully actualized' is the correct rendering of 'fully actualized potentiality,' for either one of them would allow us to attribute potentiality to a God whose simplicity precludes his having any. Hence, the God who

4. P. T. Geach, *Reference and Generality* (Ithaca: Cornell University Press, 1980, 3d ed.), 142–51.

is Pure Actuality can contain no potentiality, ability, or capacity, not even ones that are fully actualized, fully exercised, or fully extended respectively.

Once we grasp that even fully actualized potentiality is completely alien to the notion of Pure Actuality, it is clear that it simply makes no sense to speak of God as having any ability or capacity to do or to be anything. Nor, of course, does it make any sense to say that he has any *in*ability or *in*capacity to be or to do anything. In fact, the dichotomies ability/inability, capacity/incapacity, potentiality/nonpotentiality have no more application to God than the dichotomy moral/immoral has to a raindrop. Consequently, we need to be discerning if we wish to apply to God the scholastic tag *ab esse ad posse valet illatio*. Applying it to the fact that Socrates *is F*, we can infer 'Socrates *can* be *F*.' Applying it to the fact that God is *F*, however, we certainly cannot infer 'God *can* be *F*': all that we can infer is 'It can be that (God is *F*).' In other words, internal or *de re* necessity and possibility are quite inapplicable to the God who is Pure Actuality: the only necessity and possibility applicable to him are external or *de dicto*.

Since it makes no sense to attribute any ability at all to Pure Actuality, a fortiori it makes no sense to attribute to him any ability to change. So, God is immutable, which is of course far from saying that he is inactive. And, being immutable, there can be no question of his interacting with his creatures, as process theologians are wont to think that he does.

Finally, to have recognized these various implications of God's being Pure Actuality is to be freed from the illusion of there being any way at all of conceiving him as a human being writ large. Rather, it is to be committed to thinking about him in a number of new and decidedly non-anthropomorphic ways, some of which I shall briefly recall.

God's Actions Ad Extra

As noted earlier, it is somewhat anomalous of Anselmians to acknowledge God as a creator, and yet to equip him with the very kind of power which would deny him all possibility of creating anything at all, the kind of power that can only be exercised *on* things. On the contrary, so far as the simplicity doctrine is concerned, there is no such anomaly, since the power attributed to God is a *limit case* of instances of human productive activity, a power that cannot be exercised *on* anything whatever. Hence, if a God who is Pure Actuality brings it about that a universe exists, it is *necessary* that he do so ex nihilo: there is just no other way he could do it. For the same reason, a God who is Pure Actuality cannot act *on* the Universe even to conserve it. Even in regard to conservation, his activity is necessarily creative. And, since his creative activity can never be exercised *on* anything, neither can it be resisted or frustrated by anything.

Exactly the same point can be made in regard to what some might conceive of as God's acting *on* individual creatures. What is mistakenly, and anthropomorphically, spoken of as God's acting *on* b to bring about F ought properly to be spoken of as God's bringing it about that (b do F). By external causation God can bring about whatever he wants b to do, albeit without acting *on* b.

Furthermore, in not acting on b, God in no way infringes on b's own causality: b is not reduced to being a divine puppet. And, since he does not infringe on b's own causality, a fortiori he does not infringe on b's *free* causality, should b be a free agent. This became clear in chapter 7.

What If God Had Not Created the Universe?

Since it was not necessary that God create the Universe, it was possible that he not create. It might therefore be suggested that he would surely have had the potentiality to create, and hence could not be Pure Actuality. Surely not. Although unquestionably an insuperable problem if Pure Actuality were conceived of as merely a being in which all potentialities were actualized, it is no threat to Pure Actuality conceived of as totally lacking in potentiality. The brief reason is that, if God has no potentiality at all—whether actualized or unactualized—then of course he could never have had any unexercised potentiality such as the potentiality to create the Universe.

This would seem puzzling only if we were to insist on using modal operators internally in comparing two situations in the following ways:

> God actually creates the Universe.
> Even if God had not created the Universe, he could nevertheless have done so.

If those propositions really did depict the two situations correctly, then a God who did not create would undoubtedly have an unactualized potentiality. For a simple God, however, the two situations can be depicted only by using modal operators externally:

> Actually (God creates the Universe)
> Even if God had not created the Universe, it was possible that (God create the Universe)

The external use of 'it is possible' imputes no potentiality to God: it merely makes the unexceptionable point that creating the Universe is not inconsistent with God's being God.

Freedom without Choice

A God who is Pure Actuality is not to be conceived of as making a choice after weighing up the competing merits of creating one universe rather than another, or perhaps creating none at all. That would be to conceive of him as *being able* to do each of these things, as having the potentiality to do them, and even to change his mind about doing them. And that, in turn, would be to say that Pure Actuality was not Pure Actuality. As we have seen, it is simply false to say 'God could create the Universe,' and for the same reason it is also false to say 'God could change his mind about creating the Universe.'

Although the internal use of 'could' in 'God could create the Universe' imputes potentiality to God, its external use does not. It is therefore perfectly proper to say, 'It could be that (God create the Universe)' as well as 'It could be that (God not create the Universe).' Not only do these impute no potentiality to God, they do not impute any choice to him either. A fortiori, they impute to him no possibility of his changing his mind. They do, however, make clear that 'God creates the Universe' is not a necessary proposition, and hence that God is not bound to create the Universe: he does so freely. Although choice may entail freedom, freedom entails neither choice nor the possibility of a change of mind.

God's Willing and Knowing[5]

Because God has no potentiality, it would be as much a logical howler to say 'God necessarily wills his own goodness' or 'God contingently wills to create the Universe' as it would be to say 'God can will his own goodness' or 'God can will to create the Universe.' Once again, the reason is that modal operators cannot be used internally in talk about a simple God. In regard to God's willing, therefore, the correct thing to say is, 'Necessarily (God wills his own goodness)' and 'Contingently (God wills to create the Universe).' To say that both are true is, however, not to say that there are two willings in God, one necessary and the other contingent. On the contrary, there is no multiplicity of willings, but only a multiplicity of truths relating to the one willing, e.g.,

9.05. God wills (both his own goodness and to create the Universe).
9.06. God's goodness is an object of the divine will in every possible world. (This proposition is therefore a necessary one.)

---

5. The contents of this section have been developed at much greater length in responding to objections against the divine simplicity in the Appendix to Chapter 5.

9.07.   God's creation of the Universe is an object of the divine will in less than every possible world. (Because it holds in less than every possible world, this proposition is a contingent one.)

The misconception of Pure Actuality that prompted the view of God as having at least two willings is also precisely the misconception underlying the view that he has at least two knowings—one in necessarily knowing himself and the other in contingently knowing the Universe. But God no more has two knowings than he has two willings. There is no multiplicity of divine knowings, only a multiplicity of truths about that knowing, e.g.,

9.08.   God knows everything about (both himself and the Universe).
9.09.   God himself is an object of the divine knowing in every possible world. (This proposition is a necessary one.)
9.10.   The Universe is an object of the divine knowing in less than every possible world. (This proposition is a contingent one.)

Conclusion

It is now clear that even an understanding of God as the zero-bound instance of existence, as Pure Actuality, and as identical with each of his properties can be dangerously superficial unless accompanied by a recognition that many of the ordinary ways of conceiving of him are in fact gross misconceptions which, though perfectly appropriate to creatures, are quite outlandish as applied to God. Consequently, we need to be sensitive to the inconsistency in attributing choice to the being who is Pure Actuality, or in attributing to him any abilities corresponding to any of his properties. It may seem innocent enough to say that a God who has the property of knowing has also the *ability* to know, and similarly for other properties. Yet, although these attributions are all entirely appropriate to creatures, they are absurd as applied to God.

True, God does know, understand, will, and create, but he does so without engaging any correlative ability. Likewise, although he is free, he exercises that freedom without engaging any ability to choose. So, when we accept that he differs absolutely from creatures, we need to be aware of exactly what that precludes us from saying. In particular, it precludes most of the claims made so freely by perfect-being theologians, who seem to have no qualms about depicting God as making *choices*, as having the *ability* to create a universe different from our own, as one whose creative activity, knowledge, and understanding are the exercise of his *abilities* to create, know, and understand respectively, and who acts *on* his creatures as they themselves act on each other, albeit rather less powerfully and less efficaciously than their creator. Anselmians are so far under the spell of anthropomorphism as to fail to realise that this way of depicting the creator of the Universe is not merely false, it is positively bizarre.

If our portrait has been distinctive in depicting God as having neither abilities nor potentialities of any kind, it is distinctive also in denying any difference between the divine attributes which the Anselmian's portrait is at pains to distinguish so sharply. The fact is that Pure Actuality is Pure Intelligence, is Pure Wisdom, is Pure Benevolence, and so on for all the divine attributes. Their lack of distinction, however, does not prevent our recognizing relations between them and each of the human-like attributes that perfect-being theologians like to consider as divine. This is not to deny the identity between the former but simply to acknowledge that the entity which itself lacks any internal distinction is the common *limit case* instance of many attributes that are so diverse in creatures. Moreover, the very fact that the uncaused cause of the Universe is the common limit case of all the pure perfections suffices to show that he is worthy of worship. And that brings us to the end of that journey which Hepburn professed to find so problematic, the journey 'from uncaused cause to the worship-worthy God of Christian religion.'[6]

The doctrine of the divine simplicity has therefore proved not only to be entirely intelligible and defensible, but to be crucial in making available to us an understanding of God as being transcendent in a way that, for different reasons, has so eluded Anselmians and negative theologians alike. What they, and process theologians too, have thought to be a most unlikely God is in fact the God who created us.[7]

6. Previously quoted in the Preface.

7. This God, the God of the philosophers, is also the God of the Bible. I say this because, being a creator, the God of the Bible could be nothing if not simple; and there can be only one simple God. To the objection that the Bible not only makes no mention of his simplicity but speaks of him in a thoroughgoing anthropomorphic way, I reply that this is scarcely surprising, for the Bible is no more a philosophical treatise than it is a scientific one. We have no more right to expect it to describe God in philosophical terms than to describe the origin of the Universe in scientific terms. To have done either of these things would have been to subvert completely the very purposes for which the Bible was written.

Index

knowings
  only one act in God, 103
  zero-bound limit case of, 89–91
Kretzmann, N., 123n
  on identity between divine properties,
    118

Langtry, B., viii
Leftow, B., viii
  on intrinsic state of divine knowledge,
    99–101
  on quasi-Molinism, 124–25
Leftow's second option, 125–26
  criticism, 127
Leibniz, G., 3
limit case, 4, 161–62
  of bound of existence, is zero-
    bounding, 63
  instance of bound of existence, 44
  instance of existence, 61–69
  of more than one series, 82
  notion of, 7–10, 81
  of property instances, 71, 115
  unrecognized by perfection-being the-
    ology, 10
'limit case,' an alienans adjective, 10, 66,
  81, 99, 116
limit simpliciter, 4, 7, 85
Lombard, Peter, on creation, 130n
Londey, D., 20–21, 27
Loux, M., viii

Maimonides, M.
  on controlling notion of God, 3
  on divine simplicity, 11
  on negative theology, 4–7
Mann, W.
  on Aquinas, 85n
  on divine cognition, 99n
  on God as a rich property, 75
Mavrodes, G., 89n
mere conservationism, 128
middle knowledge. *See* Molina
modal operators, external mandatory for
  simple God, 98–108 *passim*, 165–66
modal uniformity problem, 108–12
Molina
  on middle knowledge, 123–24

  on foreknowledge and human free-
    dom, 139–40
Mondin, B., on analogy, 144
Morris, T. V.
  on co-extension of divine properties,
    117
  on God's sharing creaturely proper-
    ties, 116–17
  on great-making properties, 1–2
  on negative theology, 14n
  on omniscience, 96–99
  on problem of modal uniformity,
    107–12
  on Subsistent Existence, 75

names, fictional and empty, 11n
necessity, relative-temporalized (*RT*), 47,
  140n
negation, internal and external, 23–25
  passim
negative existential propositions, 22–23
  paradox of, 20–21
negative theology
  on notion of God, 4–7, 142, 158
  on God-talk, 154
Nielsen, K., objection to analogy, 149–50
non-existence, 18, 21, 23
  is a Cambridge property, 21, 24, 26, 27

occasionalism, 89, 128
Ogden, S., necessity and contingency in
  God, 127
omnipotence
  limit case of power, 89, 115
  most profound meaning of, 87–89
omniscience
  notion of, 91, 98–99
  what it does not imply, 96–98
on/off character of existence, 40–41

Pailin, D., on divine attributes, 3n
paradox of perfection, 114
particular causes. *See* cause
'perfect' as an alienans adjective, 119
perfect being, notions of, 1–5
perfect-being theology, vii, 1–4, 81–95,
  159–60
  anthropomorphism of, 3, 85, 159–60

About the Author

Barry Miller is an Honorary Fellow at the University of New England, Armidale, Australia. This book is a sequel to his *From Existence to God* (1992), which argued in detail for the existence of a creator of the universe.